Granite
and Grace

seeking
the heart of
Yosemite

Michael P. Cohen

Illustrations by Valerie P. Cohen

UNIVERSITY OF NEVADA PRESS *Reno & Las Vegas*

University of Nevada Press | Reno, Nevada 89557 USA

www.unpress.nevada.edu

Copyright © 2019 by University of Nevada Press
Chapter openers and frontispiece art © 2019 Valerie P. Cohen

Cover art by Brian Welker | Dreamstime.com

Cover design by Matt Strelecki

All photos are by the author unless otherwise indicated.

LIBRARY OF CONGRESS CATALOGING-IN-PUBLICATION DATA

Names: Cohen, Michael P., 1944- author.

Title: Granite and grace : seeking the heart of Yosemite / Michael P. Cohen.

Description: Reno ; Las Vegas : University of Nevada Press, [2019] |
  Identifiers: LCCN 2018052825 (print) | LCCN 2018056616 (ebook) | ISBN
  9781948908177 (ebook) | ISBN 9781948908160 (pbk. : alk. paper)

Subjects: LCSH: Granite--California--Yosemite National Park. |
  Geology--California--Yosemite National Park. | Natural
  history--California--Yosemite National Park. | Tuolumne Meadows (Calif.) |
  Cohen, Michael P., 1944- | Hikers--Biography. |
  Hiking--California--Yosemite National Park.

Classification: LCC QE462.G7 (ebook) | LCC QE462.G7 C65 2019 (print) | DDC
  552/.3--dc23

LC record available at https://lccn.loc.gov/2018052825

FIRST PRINTING

Manufactured in the United States of America

Granite and Grace

"Mt. Conness, May 24." India Ink 20" × 30"
Valerie P. Cohen

Valerie again,
collaborator,
co-conspirator,
lover.

Contents

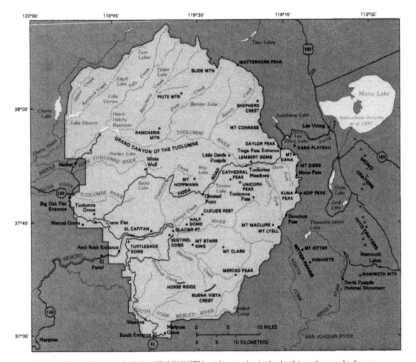

YOSEMITE NATIONAL PARK AND VICINITY—index map showing key localities and geographic features.

FIGURE I.1. Simplified Yosemite map. Source: Norman King Huber (1926–2007), *The Geologic Story of Yosemite National Park* (Washington: Government Printing Office, 1987). USGS Bulletin 1595

Introduction

THIS MODEST SET of essays explores our nearly lifelong experiment to experience and respond to the granite of a region called Tuolumne Meadows in Yosemite National Park (figure 1). Other than remarkable granite forms, many aspects of this place have attracted us over the years, not the least of which is the community of people who are also drawn to the region. But we came and lived here as much as we could to expose ourselves to granite, to feel and explore it, and to explore ourselves. Tuolumne Meadows provided a place for us to think and feel. This book tests our nonscientific experiments.

While walking on trails in national parks, it is not surprising to overhear people who spend most of their time talking not about where they are, but about concerns from where they come, as if they cannot afford to pay full attention to the present rock on which they tread. When Valerie and I desire to persuade these hikers to change we are immediately faced by a strange paradox. We have only ourselves as solitary exemplars and must speak about ourselves, not only where we are. As Henry David Thoreau so famously wrote, "I should not talk so much about myself if there were anybody else whom I knew as well."[1]

This book intends to avoid the so-called "wilderness controversy" despite the prominence of solitary experience here, which would seem to reveal traditional wilderness predilections.[2] The institutional construction of the Wilderness Act of 1964 embedded within it a concept of solitude, defining wilderness areas in part as affording "outstanding opportunities for solitude or a primitive and unconfined type of recreation."[3] Nevertheless, the concept of solitude is much older and more nuanced than the American conservation movement's version of it, and I refer to that more venerable concept when I speak of solitude.

When "a person longs for solitude and at the same time is fearful of it," the Hungarian translator, critic, and art critic F. László Földényi argues, such a person may become a prisoner of that longing.[4] Solitude might also make him free. How to separate a desire for solitude from ideological issues, a desire for privacy, or even a predilection toward melancholy? Földényi insists that solitude, silence, and melancholy are wrapped inextricably around each other: "A melancholic wishes, first and foremost, to escape *from himself*, but he can find no crack in the homogeneous, overarching culture, and resignation grows in him, together with a sense of helplessness. In the end, he petrifies inwardly as well, feeling he has been robbed of his capacity for both wanting and not wanting."[5]

Yet Kierkegaard, in one instance, believed that living in solitude would allow a person to find a way back to the basic principles of life.[6] Földényi concludes his book *Melancholy*: "With every step he takes, man tries to smuggle some goal into nothingness. The melancholic is skeptical of those goals."[7]

Even John Muir received plenty of advice about the costs of solitude and the value of sociability. Emerson once wrote to him that "there are drawbacks also to Solitude, who is a sublime mistress, but an intolerable wife."[8] Perhaps too much solitude is not good for anyone, but every age must ask how much is too much and when a desire for solitude becomes pathological.

It is true I often enjoy being alone, and sometimes in the past I enjoyed climbing mountains solo, but only on very straightforward routes. These were typically day-long excursions. I have never enjoyed being alone for longer and prefer to return to social circumstances every evening. However, just because the framers of the Wilderness Act emphasized solitude as part of the experience of wilderness doesn't mean that those who seek solitude desire a wilderness experience. For instance, Valerie and I enjoy taking a walk quietly, somewhere not filled with horseplay, not because we are looking for "wilderness" but because it is pleasant in itself. I find my commerce with rock, especially granite, best transacted without conversation, because I desire something concrete and immediate, not articulate and meaningful.

Writing these narratives cannot follow directly from our walking. In writing, I follow a method the art critic John Berger endorses in *Ways of Seeing* (1972) and that Walter Benjamin originally articulated in "The Work of Art in the Age of Mechanical Reproduction."[9] I imagine that each of Tuolumne Meadows' granitic domes is like a "coded testament addressed to the present."[10] And who feels or listens, and who shall tell the story of encountering these rocks? According to Benjamin, "[storytelling] does not aim to convey the pure essence of the thing, like information or a report. It sinks the thing into the life of the storyteller, in order to bring it out of him again." Indeed, the storyteller is the figure who encounters himself.[11]

Consequently, I am aware of many risks here. Nor have I ever trusted memoirs. Following an acute academic friend, the historian Richard White, I am highly distrustful of written memories, not only because memory can often be flawed, but also because memory is sometimes fabricated.[12] Memory forgets or erases what it does not wish to recall. "Memory is like a dog that lies down where it pleases," according to an engaging simile of Dutch writer Cees Nooteboom.[13] Please make no mistake: Though Valerie, my partner for more than fifty years, is a party to these excursions, these memories are mine alone.

What you have in your hands is unmistakably a memoir that deliberately attempts to carry our past metaphorically into the present—and also claims to be about metamorphosis. When writing engages metaphors (or similes) for memory, memory becomes metaphorical. Books themselves are a form of "external memory," not inside but outside our minds, not oral but written.[14] I claim that the granitic forms of Tuolumne Meadows constitute an external memory for us. Whether they will last longer than books remains to be seen. I'm betting on the rocks.

Generally speaking, we are also told that it is a mistake for writers or artists to attempt explanations of their lives or their works, especially in print. Nevertheless the following narratives implicate me directly, perhaps showing that I am unredeemed in my pursuits—and certainly demonstrating that I am capable of contradicting myself.

This experiment means to use the *method* of the *essai*, as Montaigne called it: a testing or trying out that subjects inner life to decisive thought. These essays are meant not only to demonstrate how we perceive and think about ourselves within this extraordinary place, but also to explore some of the influences and grounds for our ideas and perceptions.

I use the word *hard* and its synonyms a great deal in these attempts to grasp granite firmly because this word reveals a human response to unyielding rock: Encounters with rock are often difficult to endure or accomplish and offer a severe or rigorous test; its rough, coarse, harsh textures are hard on the hands and often involve going the hard way.

Granite, the substance or matter that occasions this book, can be found all over the world, but what we know best appears in Yosemite National Park. It is next to impossible to write anything original about Yosemite, not only because so much has been written, but also because so much has been overwritten.

Yosemite has occasioned some very good writing on geology across a set of literary-scientific texts. This tradition's main figures include Josiah D. Whitney, John Muir, Grove Karl Gilbert, François Matthes, N. King Huber, and the current park geologist, Greg Stock. These literary texts are in some ways like a palimpsest, each successively written over previous versions. My writing falls within the context of that tradition but does not pretend to be scientific in any modern, professional, or technical sense—nor do I claim to establish a history of Yosemite's geological writing or to conclude this tradition.

Because I have written about John Muir extensively—and also because Muir's Yosemite is overwritten in several senses— I invoke his description:

> Of this glorious range [the Sierra Nevada] the Yosemite National Park is a central section, thirty-six miles in length and forty-eight miles in breadth. The famous Yosemite Valley lies in the heart of it, and it includes the head waters of the Tuolumne and Merced rivers, two of the most songful streams in the world; innumerable lakes and waterfalls and smooth silky lawns; the noblest forests, the loftiest granite domes, the deepest ice-sculptured cañons, the brightest crystalline pavements, and snowy mountains soaring into the sky twelve and thirteen thousand feet, arrayed in open ranks and spiry pinnacled groups partially separated by tremendous cañons and amphitheatres; gardens on their sunny brows, avalanches thundering down their long white slopes, cataracts roaring gray and foaming in the crooked rugged gorges, and glaciers in their shadowy recesses working in silence, slowly completing their sculpture; new-born lakes at their feet, blue and green, free or encumbered with drifting icebergs like miniature Arctic Oceans, shining, sparkling, calm as stars.[15]

Talk about overwrought metaphors for memory! Perhaps we can forgive the confident tone of *Our National Parks*, as a man in his sixties celebrates the accomplishments of his generation of conservationists. Aside from Muir's mention of noble forests, songful streams, gardens, and silky lawns, he highlights most of all his geological memories of lofty granite, soaring mountains, and rugged gorges. This has been a safe bet for other writers.

Muir narrates some memories more intimately in *My First Summer in the Sierra*, his re-collected journals of excursions around Tuolumne Meadows in 1869. From his base camp near Soda Springs, "The sublime, massive Mt. Dana and its companions, green, red, and white, loom impressively above the pines along the eastern horizon; a range or spur of gray rugged granite crags and mountains on the north; the curiously crested and battlemented Mt. Hoffman on the west; and the Cathedral Range on the south." The meadows themselves he calls "full of sunshine like a lake of light."[16] Muir's overwrought Yosemite has petrified into a nearly archetypal written memoir. In many ways, his Yosemite is our own—but not entirely.

We must own certain differences. For instance, those who have become concerned about the biological health of wildlife living in Yosemite have been fighting a losing battle for many decades. Though the National Park Service claims as many as 80 species of mammals, 250 species of birds, 1,400 kinds of flowering plants, and 37 species of trees including the giant sequoia, the prognosis for their continuing health is not good. As the Park Service itself has announced, "The diversity of native species, including the genetic material they contain, the natural processes with which they are critically intertwined, and the corridors by way of which they move, are declining at a historically unprecedented rate."[17]

We are not optimistic about preserving biological diversity in Yosemite or anywhere else, nor can one find many sanguine experts.[18] Under such diminished circumstances, the rock Muir praised is likely to be the longest lasting legacy of his national park. This granite rock's endurance is more than metaphorical, though it has certainly fulfilled that function in the work of writers like Gary Snyder and Robinson Jeffers.

There are myriad ways to travel on Muir's granitic domes and peaks; I tried as many as I could without falling off. Valerie and I spent several spring and fall seasons climbing rocks in Yosemite Valley, migrating to the domes and spires of Tuolumne Meadows each July when it became too warm in the Valley. Eventually we found the topography of Tuolumne Meadows more congenial and ceased to enter the Valley at all.

The intention of these essays is topographic. By topography, I mean a description of a place, from the Greek *topos*, literally place, region, or space; and *graphein*, to write, express, or represent by written characters, or perhaps by drawn lines. Broadly speaking, a local topography includes not only relief—depicted through contour lines on the United States Geological Survey topographical quadrangles—but also natural and artificial features and even local history and culture.

There are now no secret places in Tuolumne Meadows. Almost everything a visitor to Tuolumne might desire can be located on specialized maps, climbers' and hikers' guides, the internet, or Google maps. These include climbing routes, legal and illegal camping spaces, and directions for hiking to landmarks, viewpoints, and interesting sites. We use more traditional methods for orienting ourselves—literary works and especially older maps. We always carry a topographical map.

Geologic maps depict in idealized form the distribution of materials at or near the ground surface of the Earth. As produced by the USGS, geologic maps for Yosemite are superimposed on base topographical maps, with each different geologic unit (for example, Cathedral Peak Granodiorite) listed on an accompanying legend and printed in a distinct color.[19] Because the base map is printed in light colors, the effect for the reader is a flattening of the plane, very like the flattening of the picture plane in the work of modern painters who aimed to call attention to the creation of an artifact. Geologic maps call attention to themselves as two-dimensional surfaces. In this regard, they are strange beasts—they are layered, so to speak, in reverse, with geology on top of topography.[20] Perhaps that is why I have a sense, when reading them, that geologic information is being superimposed over my topographical sense.[21] We never carry geologic maps on our walks. We are informed by them at home, but outdoors we seek what is not on them.

Perhaps because we have always consulted books and maps, we never thought of Yosemite's rock as a "frontier," where one could, like Huckleberry Finn, "light out for the Territory ahead of the rest," as if engaged in some exchange of civilization for freedom.[22] Does an unclimbed rock seem like a frontier? I think not. Climbing on granite is a highly civilized activity that requires physical preparation, paying close attention, judging geological suitability, establishing techniques and technology, and logistical planning. Rock climbers sometimes speak of *gardening* routes by cleaning vegetation out of cracks. This practice is more common in Yosemite Valley and is not, in my experience, necessary for climbs in Tuolumne Meadows.

From a distance these domes and cliffs may all look the same, but they are all different underfoot. Many look featureless, but they are not. I am particularly interested in what one scholar describes as "the haptic process by which climbers comprehend and experience place."[23] Haptic: pertaining to the sense of touch.

Stories of lighting out for the territory in Yosemite and in Mono County, where we reside for half of each year, typically end up being stories of loss and failure, as Valerie learned while serving as a ranger for the National Park Service. Nor do we believe that the interior west, as in Mono County, will be successful in attempting to live by the tourist industry in the long run. Yosemite by night too frequently consists of someone in a motel room or a tent, crying. Valerie has many stories of dislocated people whose urban troubles amplified when they came to the parks, but this is not the right place for these stories.

When Yosemite National Park was created as part of an imperial and exclusionary impulse, it displaced native inhabitants. Since then, Yosemite National Park has been an enclosed space dedicated to benefit people other than the original inhabitants. Nearly a century before we were born, Euro-Californians said to the native inhabitants of the region, "This is our land, not yours."

In the course of this process, white American visitors and settlers renamed landmarks. In Tuolumne Meadows this often proceeded frivolously, people naming landmarks after their heroes, themselves, their relatives, their friends and associates, and even stray domestic animals. Such names as Polly Dome, Dog Dome, and Puppy Dome remain. Climbers later named some domes with even less respect, as in Whizz Domes and Drug Dome. Some names are associated with arbitrary political divisions, as in Mariuolumne Dome, on the border of Mariposa and Tuolumne counties. Some domes have been named according to directions from the Tioga Road, as with Daff Dome (an acronym for "Dome Across From Fairview"). Consequently, guides to the region are often keyed to the mileage on a modern highway that only sometimes traces traditional indigenous routes, as if geography follows the choices of engineers. Some name changes indicate competing interests. The dome that Muir named Glacier Monument became Fairview Dome.[24] Steve Roper decided to rename a portion of Polly Dome "Stately Pleasure Dome" in his *The Climber's Guide to the High Sierra*.[25]

These names are continuing reminders that Yosemite is a recently dispossessed landscape, as Susan Schrepfer demonstrates in *Nature's Altars*.[26] In *Dispossessing the Wilderness: Indian Removal and the Making of the National Parks*, Mark David Spence holds that "if Yosemite National Park teaches us anything, it is that scenes of great permanence are fraught with historical change."[27]

Scholars such as Gary Fields at UC San Diego have been involved in investigating this issue on an international scale in places like Palestine. As Fields expresses it, territorial landscapes dramatize the power of dominant groups to reorganize all dimensions of lives in particular places; he asks, "How does landscape itself become an instrument of force in this process of transformation?"[28] These questions can and should be applied to Yosemite, but that is not our purpose here.

Yosemite's imperial history has made it a monumental task to validate original names for landmarks—and not only because names are metaphorical. The origins of the names *Tuolumne* and *Yosemite*, for instance, have been contested for decades. The varied and conflicting accounts of their sources are not entirely reliable, though both names are undoubtedly corruptions of indigenous ones. Nor are they likely to undergo substitution, as may happen with Tis-sa-ack for Half Dome, or has already with Denali for Mt. McKinley. So-called "legends"—as recounted in the lore of commercial tourism, which is sometimes parroted by the National Park Service and then attached to landmarks—are arguably unreliable. They are almost all condescending and often corrupt, which is to say destructive of significance. None are particularly helpful in understanding the historical past of the original residents of this region. In this and in a larger sense, Yosemite's history continues to be contested.[29] We await better ways for visitors to learn about the region's historical past.

But to speak more personally, Valerie and I did not learn to name or perceive the landmarks of Yosemite through native language or native eyes, and there is no point in pretending that we did. We use here the names we were taught, or at most substitute names from our own culture.

My cultural background has been both literary and scientific. According to Aristotle, whose definition most literary theorists accept, a metaphor uses a "strange name" to accomplish a "transfer of meaning" to a different context.[30] Certainly this process of using strange names to transfer meaning also occurs extensively in the languages of geologists. I appropriate a great deal of that geological transference in what follows. When these essays use strange names for rocks, however, meaning is meant to be transferred to more than geology.

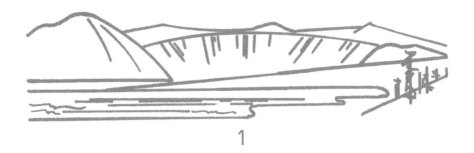

Invocation:
Going to Granite

Valerie and I walk to the Granite Lakes.

VALERIE AND I have been going to Gaylor and Granite Lakes for fifty years. Though we have approached from several directions, we now start from outside the east entrance—the back door of Yosemite Park—at ten thousand feet of altitude, so that we do not have to sit in a long line where we have seen people crying in their cars while waiting to enter.

Leaving our car, we ascend the ridge above Tioga Pass, stepping through a variety of broken rock—sandstone, siltstone, conglomerate, and volcanic—before we overlook an open basin. We turn our back on Dana's massive hunk of mostly red metamorphic rock (Metamorphosed Sedimentary and Volcanic Rocks, according to the geologic map) and descend to find what has arisen from under these older rocks, known by geologists as a roof pendant.[1]

Then it is a familiar stroll for us across alluvium and glacial deposits. This walk does not get old, worn, or boring. I first came here as a child, about ten years before meeting Valerie, by following Carl Sharsmith, Tuolumne Meadows ranger naturalist. That summer I also followed him up Mount Dana.

There is nothing exceptional about our journey, or else it is all exceptional. For one thing, as soon as we ascend a rise called Gaylor Pass, we can see a large portion of the geology of

Tuolumne Meadows. Middle Gaylor Lake, one of three, is itself an infinity pool and marks only the beginning of our tour, because we are going to granite. Seeing Mounts Dana and Gibbs, Kuna Crest, Kuna Lakes, places we shared with many friends, too numerous to name. What does it mean to share? one might wonder. We wish to acknowledge this as a public place, apportioned to all of us, that includes feelings enjoyed or suffered with others.

As we move out of the metamorphic, toward a granite cirque, we can read this transition like a familiar book, a classic we have enjoyed these many years. More of the roof pendant is visible to the south; Mounts Lyell and McClure (I prefer McClure) are always on the southern horizon. We have been to their summits. We point out other journeys on granite, Amelia Earhart, Vogelsang, and Johnson Peaks; Echo, Cathedral, and Unicorn Peaks; and more.

These are some of our landmarks. We cherish these poles of our known and eternal wanderings and indulge ourselves in viewing them. We have traveled up, down, and around, each excursion providing its own delights. This bowl of rock holds our pleasure; much of what counts in our marriage has endured as a result of walking in these places.

We have seen wildlife here: bears, coyotes, marmots, Clark's nutcrackers, hummingbirds, Belding's ground squirrels, lupine, wallflower, phlox, paintbrush, lodgepole pine, whitebark pine, and so on. Mostly, we have seen ourselves here, ambling over ridges, stopping for snacks, swatting mosquitoes. We rest on familiar granite blocks and under old trees.

I have picked up arrowheads, caught trout, eaten lunch, and watched snow melt in these spaces—and listened to stories worth knowing. My father used to fish here; his short legs took him to one of his favorite places, Upper Gaylor Lake. Sheridan Anderson, who taught Valerie about ink drawing, also took Valerie's mother fishing here.

We imagine that this place is still largely unchanged, the same every year—though we know this is not true. Permanence is supposedly part of what it means to be in a national park, to be in a place that means to last longer than an individual human life, at least. It is a relief to come here and know some stability in the world, though not enough. We meet many more people than we used to, sometimes with difficulty. Yet we are happy to meet those who love these places. But we do not come here for social reasons now. Instead, we come earlier in the morning to have some solitude.

After traversing a jumble of sedimentary and metamorphic rocks and crossing a good deal of ground-up glacial deposit, we approach Granite Lakes. Finally coming to bedrock, we release our breaths. We have been seeking this place purely for comfort and pleasure: to enter a realm that seems almost magical, something solid in our travels that calms the soul, reminds us of what is permanent and what is ephemeral. No doubt it seems this way because the rock here has been glaciated.

After our trudge across rough glacial deposits, the granite smoothed by glaciers seems remarkably solid and unsullied. We have entered a geological region known as the Tuolumne Intrusive Suite. To be more precise, the rock on which we sit is named Granodiorite of Kuna Crest. Call it granite. Who's here to correct you? We are in a small basin where rock, water, and alpine greenery meet. Our voices echo from a cirque above.

Whatever we name this rock, the place remains the same. It is a constant in our lives, like many other places we visit in this region. These rough and smooth shapes are central because they reveal an essential map of our world, and we respect it. This is not our place, but rather someplace we belong to and always will. We love each other in part because we love this place in which we are together. When we accept this landscape as a link that joins us to each other, there is nothing natural about our choice.

I mention this triangular connection in spite of the fact that what follows is not about our nearly lifelong commitment to each other, but mostly focuses on my own personal relationship with granite. Valerie and I are not deluded that we are first to see and appreciate these granite shapes. These rocks rise above us to our west as we sit for a snack and watch fish rise from the clear water of Lower Granite Lake. Valerie has many thoughts about this place for she has painted and sketched here many times, as have painters before her—like Chiura Obata, whose *Lake Basin in the High Sierra* we believe is an image of this lake with cliffs beyond.[2]

Being no painter, I have a different relationship to this place and come into the presence of this rock with hand, foot, and mind. Sometime after I was introduced to this region I became a rock climber, and now have turned to a more leisurely relation to these places. Many of my climbing partners are gone, and those who remain have mostly ceased to spend time in the mountains.

And no wonder. Here in the present, trees of California, and especially of the Sierra Nevada, are dying. As our climate changes, fire suppressed for generations now sweeps forests. This kind of change in the forests is not unprecedented. But the causes of these changes, beyond natural cycles of climate, are human. Many remaining forests appear ghostly now, as the pine needles turn brown and then gray. We all know this.

The old Sierra Club wilderness activists used to speak of the Forest Service's proposals for "starfish wilderness" areas or "wilderness on the rocks," which protected only high ridges extending out from peaks, but not the forests and biota below. David Brower spoke for something more comprehensive that would include "corridors that were the living space, that were the setting, where you would stay and live and enjoy yourself and look up at the peaks."[3]

But the rocks are not dying. The rocks have a different history and fate. Therefore, in these dark times I have made a compact to have commerce with rock. It has come to this: Of the many aspects of the world to which one might become attached, the most secure is granite.

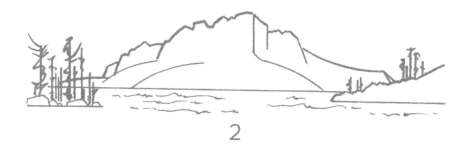

2

Human Bodies

I experience granite by walking upon it.

The mind can neither imagine anything,
nor recollect past things,
except while the body endures.

SPINOZA[1]

SOMETIMES I AWAKEN before dawn, and before the small daily pains of getting up and about, I lie in bed remembering climbs I have attempted and people I have partnered with, their faces in the sun, the scars on my hands, a bit of fear and a bit of pleasure. But this awakening to memory seems still like a dream, where the only real part is played by rock itself. Granite.

Once I am awake, I ask two questions: "What can one learn from granite—what does it reveal about being in the world?" and "What can one learn from granite's relations to the world in which it appears?" These are separate but tangled questions in my mind, and perhaps in the minds of others. As for the former question: I believe that I have learned a great deal about my own body and mind while clambering, climbing, running, and walking upon—living with—granite. Indeed, I acquired a sense of my body's possibilities when I began to travel the Sierra Nevada on foot.

I might also say that when facing austerity, perhaps one learns patience from the granite of these mountains. As for rock itself, I take it to be a surface—a crust of Earth where I initiate intimate contact with the body of the world. All my life I have attempted facing up to rock while also critiquing my style of encountering it. By style I mean a human approach toward expression. The very term *encounter* is not quite right, since it suggests meeting an adversary. Geologists frequently say they encounter certain problematic formations, and climbers are certainly prone to articulate their relations with rock as encounters. I would rather say that Valerie and I are engaged with granite.

People often speak of Yosemite's granite forms as expressing austerity, which is to say they are severe, harsh, or cruel and, in particular, dry or arid. Climbers speak of El Capitan as a vertical desert. One must carry one's water on rock climbs in Yosemite. Also, these granitic forms seem simplified, almost abstract, so that one's impressions on these rocks result not so much from what is present as from what has been removed. Not many ledges. Not many handholds or footholds, and those one finds are often small. The rock itself, cold or hot depending on the season, offers little human consolation.

Contrary to the popular literary tradition of Muir and his followers, I believe that Yosemite's granitic austerity should call out a severe, grave, and understated style—unadorned, simple, without luxuries, as if scoured by ice. An austere literary style substitutes absences for more elaborate literary structures. The aesthetic of austerity is not exactly minimal; it is not just an economy of words or composition by implication. However, for these pared-down yet massive forms of highly resistant granite, a writer might take up the minimalist strategy of reducing, paring down, or condensing through omission and absence.[2] One probably should not aspire to an arid style, but neither should one gush about granite—especially not in times like these.

Geologists continually speak of the Sierra Nevada's granite as young. Nothing in this world just is: Everything has a history. Further, one should not be surprised to discover that water is part of the deeper story of this arid granite's origin. As one geologist puts it, "Temperature and water content are the two most important parameters in the formation of granitic magma . . . The fact that most terrestrial spreading centers are subaqueous thus may aid in the formation of a thick granitic continental crust."[3]

As the mountains continue to change, no landmark or peak remains exactly the same, though the idea of a static and unchanging mountain landscape is part of our cultural legacy, an agreeable fiction. But "The blue mountains are constantly walking" according to Japanese Zen master Dōgen Zenji (1200–1253). So comments Gary Snyder in *The Practice of the Wild*.[4] Indeed, these rocks are not only walking but also leap on occasion to slough off their surfaces. What we step or climb upon comes loose sometimes and ends up a pile at the base of a cliff.

Climbers established routes with great difficulty. As these became known and repeated, we once imagined them and the rock on which they were laid out to be permanent, unchanging. We recorded these as human histories with texts and figures, photos and line drawings. We named routes, sometimes fancifully, and the landmarks upon them. Over time, we have seen many of them obliterated. Periodically, as we notice these changes, we attribute them to rockfall. So it is that humans document climbing routes with pride and those routes are erased—along with any sense of permanence.

Having spent a fair amount of time on mountainsides that no longer exist as I experienced them—most radically on Mount St. Helens, but elsewhere too and even on Yosemite's granite—I learned to pay attention to gravity and tectonics, in whose context human experiences become ephemeral. What is more, this body I inhabit has changed. I am no longer young. I continue to study and understand the relationship between human bodies and rock, but no longer in an athletic sense.

Although I spent much of my youth climbing the most difficult routes I could navigate in Yosemite Valley and Tuolumne Meadows, I have always been more engaged by long-term relations with long-lived granitic forms, the focus of my discussions here. I have never been interested in fun and games—in "ripping it up," "crushing it," or whatever expression extreme athletes use these days. I am about something else—and if I cannot call it recreation, then what?

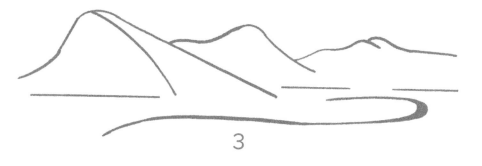

Granite Intrudes

What is granite and how is it formed?

To ask "what is this granite?" is also to ask "how, when, where, and why did it come to be here?" An intrusive igneous rock, granite is referred to as "plutonic" because it solidified at great depth, though probably not in the realm of Pluto.[1] There are about fifty identified "plutonic-rock units" in Yosemite, each consisting of one or more individual bodies of rock; the intrusive granites in the Tuolumne Intrusive Suite are among the youngest granites in Yosemite at eighty-six million years or so.[2] These have been formed by "pulses" of magmas, as they are termed, that rise, fractionate, and cool on a journey from under the crust of the Earth.

These granites are by no means Yosemite-centric. Similar and related rocks occur all down the High Sierra, on the Wheeler Crest, and in the Mono Recesses, and in many other sites of the four-hundred-mile-long and fifty-mile-wide Sierra Nevada. (There is no better introduction to the Sierra than the first chapter of John Muir's *The Mountains of California*.) All my local granites have their own origin below continental shelves. Indeed, all continents have granitic foundations. Consequently, this rock once embedded at an edge is now an exposed foundation.

Granite intrudes on thought. Here in Tuolumne Meadows, a visitor beholds granitic domes as far as the eye can see. So too there are domes all along the Sierra, some still lurking below

the surface. It is all conveniently arranged! Lembert, Fairview,
Pywiack, Polly, Medlicott, Daff, and many others with and
without names—with forests below and meadows and streams
between them. An auspicious place for a walk, in virtually any
direction. No trails needed. No wonder I am interested in how
these mountains change and stay the same every year.

No wonder someone like me would continue to hold the
somewhat absurd misconception of "ideal granite"—an arche-
type conceived as perfect. I am not alone, but my meaning is
more than geological. I look forward to meeting these granites
every year and orient myself by the fixed positions of granite
domes. The dance of change and stability here is not boring,
but entrancing. I could call these domes monuments, landmarks, or even tombstones, but they also suggest something
beyond human lives.

Even some geologists continue to subscribe to an ideal because it permits comparison, which is aided by a "conception of
an ideal magmatic granite as standard." Perhaps the "sequences
of quartz grains, potassium feldspars, and plagioclases of an
ideal magmatic granite have definite mathematical properties."[3]

Why would one seek granite, if not because it fulfills some
symmetry or ideal? Let me count the ways. It is sometimes
smooth and sometimes rough; sometimes reflects and sometimes seems to glow from within; multiple in textures, each
surface gives pleasure to the touch (usually). Granite is always
interesting and comfortingly solid to tread upon. We sit on it,
climb on it, and use its slopes for going into and coming out
of mountain lakes. Think of it as a clean rock. It is sometimes
hard to know whether we radiate or reflect its light.

Granite may be a mystery in many regards. Even geologists represent its source through imagination, writing that
"geochemically, the various types of granite can be regarded
as images of their source"—or to put it more succinctly,

"granites image their source rocks."[4] Granite images its source, and when we imagine granite we may be revealing our own origins. Granite is not ubiquitous. Distributed in a ratio of about one-to-three to basalt on Earth's surface, it is found mainly associated with continental shelves and the edges of tectonic plates. It is mostly a continental kind of rock, not the stuff of islands. If, as one might imagine, the quantity of granite on Earth has increased, so has the area of continents, and the granitic portion of Earth's surface has risen above largely basaltic ocean basins. Granite grows on us and there is more granite than there used to be.

Various schemes distinguish granites by their chemical composition and the environments in which they formed— whether derived from constituents of the crust, the mantle, or both, and as a result of continental collision, subduction, oceanic spreading, or continental doming and rifting.[5] Technical categories continue to proliferate. Our Sierra granite is one small part of the most abundant type comprising the crust.[6]

Geologists used to imagine that granite must have been intruded into the crust of the Earth during all geologic periods. Much of it is Precambrian, from an era at one time thought to precede the advent of modern life forms. In any case, granite, widely distributed throughout continental crust, is the most abundant basement rock that underlies the relatively thin sedimentary rock veneer of the continents. It is not simply a surface: It runs deep.

So we might say that Tuolumne Meadows sits at the geological center of Yosemite National Park. This central set of rocks stretches from Tower and Matterhorn Peaks, the northern peaks of what is sometimes called the roof of Yosemite, down Spiller Canyon past Whorl Mountain to the north, takes in Mount Conness and North Peak, and then dives into Yosemite Valley proper to Half Dome and Glacier Point in the south. The Tuolumne Intrusive Suite constitutes the bedrock of much, but not all, of the headwaters of the Tuolumne River. A simplified geological map of Yosemite National Park depicts it as an elongated comma, a great sigh under the west side of the crest. It constitutes the heart of Muir's Yosemite, bedrock for his *First Summer*. Some geologists speak of consanguine rock here, making the whole seem animate.

Because there are myriad variations of granite and multiple theories of its origin and because geologists have been naming species while exploring granitic origins, their sober assessment might flesh out my unreasonable fascination with this family of stone. Consider the hodge-podge of language for rocks devised by geologists; this is not my language but serves a similar literary purpose—to attach words to things.

The word *granite* names a common, widespread group of intrusive igneous rocks born of fire. These usually form at great depths and pressures under the edges of continents. The term comes from the Latin *granum*, a grain, as in the coarse-grained structure of such a crystal. What a crystal might be or how it might form has been a subject for elaborate speculation. Originally, crystals like quartz were thought to be petrified ice. Crystals—or crystal systems, to be more precise—are characterized by their symmetries. Crystals are made up of minerals, or specific chemical compounds assumed to be not originally animal or vegetable. Minerals frequently appear in crystalline form as parts of rocks that aggregate different, but often closely related, chemical compounds.

Granitic rocks, notable for their visible crystalline structures, are recognized by gradations in their mineral proportions and given names such as granite, granodiorite, tonalite, or diorite according to their visible characteristics. Granite and granodiorite, for instance, are rich in quartz; the former contains mostly potassium feldspar crystals, the latter more plagioclase (calcium and sodium) feldspar. An increasing proportion of plagioclase feldspar causes granite to pass into granodiorite. Granodiorite is darker than granite and tonalite is darker still. A rock consisting of equal proportions of ortho-clase and plagioclase feldspars plus quartz may be considered a quartz monzonite. More on these minerals later.

The term *suite* inherits the idea that igneous rocks can be *comagmatic*, defined as a collection of specimens from a single area that generally represent related igneous rocks, or a collection of specimens of a single kind that could include granites from all over the world. The names of such suites have a syntax, combining a geographic term, an adjective, and the term *suite*, as in the Tuolumne Intrusive Suite situated near the headwaters of the Tuolumne River.

Geologists speak of intrusive suites as units that have sim-ilar isotopic ages and that were probably produced during the same magmatic episode.[7] More poetically, they sometimes say that these granitic units are genetically related. These granites are intrusive upon thought, as their names lead to a mnemonic review of their sources.

Visualizing and mapping the Tuolumne Intrusive Suite from its outer edges to the core, geologists see the Granodiorite of Kuna Crest on the margin and, nesting concentrically inward, Half Dome Granodiorite, Cathedral Peak Granodiorite, and Johnson Granite Porphyry. Some but not all observers include Sentinel Granodiorite to the west. These are similar in age but also progressively younger and richer in silica as one explores in-ward. Geologists think that each came from a surge of melt from the same magma chamber and that "changes in composition re-flect various stages of fractionation and mixing of magmas."[8]

Thus the Tuolumne Intrusive Suite is "zoned" according to often subtle differences in granitic rocks; in this, the series is similar to several other intrusive suites along the Sierra's crest, these being surrounded by older granites and other country rock, as it is called. This youngest suite in Yosemite—whose exposed area comprises about 1,200 square kilometers, or a third of Yosemite National Park—was "assembled," as geologists like to say, over at least ten million years around 95 to 85 million years ago, with Half Dome Granodiorite intruding over a period approaching four million years.

In very approximate terms, these intrusions are categorized by geologists into *plutons*. As we see them in the present, *plutons* are parts of large masses whose exposed surfaces extend many hundreds of square miles; each one comprises many pulses of magma. The result of these pulses is an expanse of granite of relatively homogeneous texture and composition. Such talk of origins sounds almost animate, and some geologists speak of an evolutionary rock cycle.

Igneous rocks derived from the same parent magma bear a genetic relationship known as *consanguinity*. Closely associated in space and time, occurring in similar ways, they reveal similar chemical and mineralogical characters. According to this story, to be consanguineous is to be interrelated by common ancestry, environment, and evolution. Because *comagmatic* igneous rocks bear a common set of chemical and mineralogical qualities, they are regarded as having been derived from a common parent magma.[9]

So when geologists traditionally said that these rocks were commonly interpreted to be *cogenetic*, they meant born at the same time and place, from the same material. Nevertheless, more recent research has established pretty convincingly that plutons may be assembled incrementally.[10] As one geophysicist puts it, the Tuolumne Intrusive Suite is more like a mosaic: The "vast sea of granites hosting the glaciated high country was a mosaic of bodies added to the range at many different times, not the frozen product of a single massive ocean of magma."[11] It is natural to imagine that plutons are shaped like the domes that surround us when we are in Tuolumne Meadows, or when one looks toward Half Dome from Olmsted Point. But this is imagination working—granite is always an objective correlative for something else.

Granitic plutons often occur as part of a large mass known as a batholith, or deep rock. Batholiths are almost always made of rock such as granite, diorite, or lighter rocks associated with orogeny, which is a geologist's way of saying "mountain building." A batholith is all one piece but also fragmented, the result of a complex history, and is sizable—at least one hundred square kilometers. Here, in some past, emplaced igneous intrusive (or plutonic) rocks formed from cooled magma deep in the Earth's crust. According to my *Oxford English Dictionary*, the term *magma*, for molten rock, was introduced in 1865, six years after Darwin's *The Origin of Species* was published. It is as if the Earth and life upon it became fluid at the same time.

Rock from the depths, we say: a batholith. The Sierra Nevada's one large batholith, about three hundred miles long, is made of many intrusive suites. Rather than a single entity, the granitic Sierra is more like a three-dimensional mosaic. The Sierra Nevada Batholith formed between 120 and 85 million years ago, creating part of what we now think of as our continental crust. In geological terms, this is relatively quick work.

Batholiths and plutons have nuanced histories. Thus there are many disagreements about these matters, but no disagreement about this: The Tuolumne Intrusive Suite constitutes the heart of Yosemite, spatially and aesthetically; whatever one might learn from it often applies to the Sierra more generally.

Yet as a category, the idea of a suite is problematic. W. S. Pitcher (1919–2004), a British geologist who was internationally regarded as "the leading . . . geological statesman on granites," cautions: "It could well be argued that any attempt to categorize the granite family on a natural basis is doomed to failure given the virtually infinite number of different types which might be generated in response to a variety of generative processes and source rock combinations."[12] Though classifications sound satisfying, one must also remember a warning from Eric Harold Timothy Whitten (1927–): "The concept of suites within granitoid batholiths must be treated with extreme caution . . . Without stated, necessary, and sufficient operational definitions of the parameters (and their weighting) used in suite definition, suite/s should be avoided."[13] We categorize granites on somewhat vague grounds that reveal a cultural basis.

Granitic rocks may be known by geologists by proportions of their mineral components. Pitcher charts their elaborate evolution as developing "in their contrasted tectonic niches," of which he includes five.[14] Multiple origins, multiple granites. Mountaineers like me know these by how they feel to hand or foot; the feel is constantly changing. Given so many avatars of granite, H. H. Read, another granitologist, once advised that "the best geologist is the one who has seen the most rocks."[15] In a sense, granites animate concretely the embodiments of some global process that is an abstraction.

How animate is rock? Louise Erdrich describes an experience far from my own when she writes, "Once I began to think of stones as animate, I started to wonder whether I was picking up a stone or it was putting itself into my hand. Stones are not the same as they were to me in English."[16] I am not capable of this experience, though I respect it. I have been too well indoctrinated in western science. Nevertheless, I am dazed by infinite differences embodied in massive rock.

Perhaps the notion of reincarnation would be appropriate for the origin of granite. Volcanic arcs form as the result of rising magma from the melting of the down-going tectonic plate in a subduction zone: A curved chain of volcanoes erupts in the overriding plate. They are curved, arced, as in the Pacific "ring of fire," because of the curvature of the earth. According to one expert, when one views the entire rim of the Americas, "the principal record of arc magmatism is a discontinuous alignment of deeply eroded Cretaceous granitic batholiths extending the full length of the Cordilleran orogen. Isotopic studies indicate that the granitic magmas were composed in part of juvenile mantle components and in part of recycled crustal materials."[17] In other words, granite is neither original nor recycled, but both. So, too, with what humans do with it or imagine about it.

A tiny portion of the Earth's granite has been domesticated, belongs to our households, and sometimes becomes our servant. One touches this stone in walls, curbs, and foundations. Here, too, is the stuff of tombstones, which Americans now prefer over marble for its durability. Granite—the mineral whose constituents have been eroded, buried, fused by heat and pressure—now arises, light and clean. Granite is a natural medium for monuments.

One need only look at the south face of Mount Conness, that broad and distant obelisk, its angular weathered sides gleaming white in the sun. Large feldspar chunks nubble its unglaciated granodiorite. On Mount Conness, one seizes the texture of native rock in sharp relief and remembers. The granite of Mount Conness is a reminder of both life and death: *carpe diem* and *memento mori.*

As one geologist comments, "The interpretation of granitic textures is fundamental to understanding one of the most abundant constituents of the Earth's continental crust, granodioritic plutons."[18]

So granite intrudes, floats, rises, and then becomes the crest of the Sierra (see figure 3.1). Granite intrudes upon thought;

floats yet is the foundation of all continents. This granite does not appear to be like granite elsewhere, as, for instance, like that of the Idaho Batholith and particularly the Casto Pluton in central Idaho. Yet almost all granite comes from the same dynamic of continental plates. Granite represents global forces. Granite here pretends to be timeless—and pretends to be Californian—but it is not. Inland, in Idaho, Colorado, and elsewhere, one touches other granite and in so doing feels the intersection of continental plates.

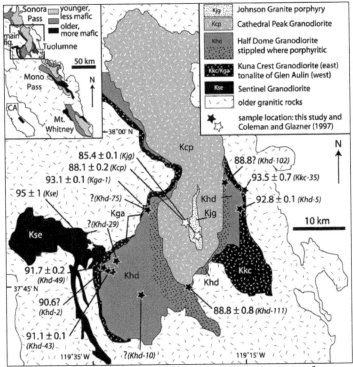

FIGURE 3.1. Simplified geology of Tuolumne Intrusive Suite after Bateman (1992). Inset shows location of Tuolumne and other Sierra Crest zoned intrusive suites. Source: Map from Drew S. Coleman et al., "Rethinking the Emplacement and Evolution of Zoned Plutons," 434. They adapt a figure from Bateman, Plutonism, Table DR1, U-Pb zircon data for rocks of Tuolumne Intrusive Suite.

Now, when one asks about the almost entirely granitic foundation of Yosemite National Park, one hears a narrative of granite evolved in plutons—masses of rock that form under the volcanoes that are so prevalent above subduction zones, where oceanic plates descend below continental plates. But only a few decades ago, when one asked where granite comes from, the answer depended on the time and place of the question.

I was first exposed to a narrative of the origin of granite while studying geochemistry in the early 1960s, when I took a job in the laboratory of George C. Kennedy at UCLA. Kennedy, who was an expert in the geochemistry of silica, proposed a history of granite and got his story wrong so that his graduate students came to refer to their studies as "Geo-whimsical Sciences." Nevertheless I was first taught to believe, as he did, that granite formed in *geosynclines*, or great troughs where sediments accumulated at the mouths of large rivers. There was something orderly and linear about his three-act story of granitic evolution: gradual concentration of silica in river deltas, deep cooking, and reemergence—a kind of placid, uniform story of redemptive geomorphology. That story is now taken to be obsolete, though Kennedy fought a rearguard battle until his end.

Plate tectonics soon revolutionized all previous theories of granitic origins. Its key principle is that the *lithosphere*, or the solid portion of the Earth's surface, has fragmented into massive, separate and distinct slabs of rock called tectonic plates, that ride on a fluid-like viscoelastic solid called the *asthenosphere*, literally a sphere of weakness. These plates converge, diverge, and collide with a kind of slow violence; their movements seem entirely contingent. There is no reason for their particular shapes or placement, but when they do collide and rub against each other, they generate huge amounts of heat. This deep and slow violence contrasts with my sense of placidity when I wander among these forms.

That my generation was taught an obsolete theory of geomorphology—and lived through a revolution in understanding the way Earth has been shaped by its history—does certainly give me pause. The genesis of granite is not so straightforward or so measured as what I was taught; now genesis is mysterious, complicated, and multiple, not as peaceful as one would like.

Consider a contrasting analogy. A weak version of biological orthogenesis proposes that the variation of organisms through successive generations in some predestined direction results in progressive evolutionary trends, independent of external factors. The strong version of biological orthogenesis proposes that an intrinsic drive slowly transforms species, so that life has an innate tendency to move in a unilinear fashion due to some internal or external "driving force." George Gaylord Simpson, the most influential paleontologist of the twentieth century, called this mechanism a "mysterious inner force."[19] Geology is driven by complex "mysterious inner forces" but no discernable goal; nor are these forces uniform in time or space across the globe. Nevertheless, the differentiation of igneous rock is a one-way street. The world of rock, in which we are guests, is both violent and placid. Rock is our home yet is often inhospitable.

What is exposed in Yosemite now calls out increasingly complicated narratives, some which perhaps illuminate global processes of continent formation all around the world. The rock of Yosemite is rough and smooth, less orderly than granite of the story I first learned. So too with our own walks.

4

Up and Down: Mountains Walking

Walking as an incomplete narrative.

And the LORD said unto Satan, Whence comest thou?
Then Satan answered the LORD, and said,
From going to and fro in the Earth,
and from walking up and down in it.

JOB 1:7

I AM NEVER DONE with walking up and down these mountains and canyons. For many years, this one certainty kept me going: believing that I would take off—to Tuolumne Peak and over Mount Hoffman, to Ragged Peak and Young Lakes, to Lyell Canyon, up Mammoth Peak, between Cathedral Peak and the Echo Peaks, striking out cross-country, following topography, letting contours of land determine an itinerary. One has to believe in something and follow some tradition: These are not paths I invented but routes I follow.

I sometimes go with others, which affects the rhythm of the experience; surely nobody need engage in an entirely solitary activity. I prefer to go with Valerie, or my dog, or with both of them; groups larger than three or four are less satisfying, in the same way that Valerie and I prefer to dine in no more than a foursome.

I am neither a prolific writer nor a fast walker. Though faster than most when going uphill, I am slower than most on flat pavement. Like many climbers of my generation, I have short legs. Our friend Chuck Pratt referred to his own as "piano stool legs." None of us are like the prodigious walkers that we read about. For instance, as Edward Hoagland puts it, "Henry Thoreau lived to write, but Muir lived to hike."[1] In this regard, though I cannot claim to emulate Thoreau or Muir, it may be that in all these fifty years I have slowly transformed myself from a walker to a writer without ceasing to walk. When one thinks of an exceptional or prodigious walker one imagines Bob Marshall. When one thinks of a prodigious climber, Norman Clyde. When one thinks of a prolific writer, who comes to mind? We nevertheless enjoy, even while growing older, a moderate version of mountain walking for the sheer physicality of it, a reminder of the animals that we have been. As our walks get shorter these days, we do not claim special wisdom or enlightenment.

We continue to walk because doing so requires going outside ourselves—to be in the world, to see the clouds, to watch the sky move, to combat self-loathing, to regain some semblance of self-respect. We live with a dog because the dog requires daily excursions, though they need not be varied or unique. As all this suggests, we are not "natural" walkers but often have to be coaxed.

I am hardly alone in this predilection. Valerie shares almost all these walks, though she no longer engages in technical climbs and has not done so for decades. Sometimes we converse, but most times we are silent. Though I cannot say for sure that she walks for the same reasons, I do know she feels about these rocks as I do. I'm also pretty sure, now that we are both in our seventies, that we come here in order to find something hopeful in a diminished world: We are alternately appalled and bored by the unending dark night of the soul, currently national and global. We walk, perhaps, to rid ourselves of a pervasive sense of loss and anger. Valerie's legs are longer than mine. Although I may sometimes be faster uphill, her legs are telling on the downhill.

I regularly reread Dōgen's text and consider his view of mountains "constantly walking," asking where he is and in which mountains. As he writes, "We must painstakingly learn in practice the virtue of this walking. The walking of mountains must be like the walking of human beings; therefore, even though it does not look like human walking, do not doubt the walking of the mountains." Some commentators depict Dōgen's mountains as blue, green, or verdant. I do not believe his were granite mountains. Dōgen insisted that the walking of mountains is "swifter than the wind, but human beings in the mountains do not sense it or know it." Most importantly, he warned, "If we doubt the walking of the mountains, we also do not yet know our own walking."[2]

Valerie does not read texts about Zen. Nevertheless, she has established her own ways of exploring the walking of mountains via her hands, using pen and ink, brush and paint. She walks across and up mountainsides, choosing her routes according to what view or tree calls to her. I look at her body of artistic work and see an increasing engagement with the dynamic of mountains, as wind and flow become the subject for more of her paintings and drawings.

Anyone might continue to puzzle over this juxtaposition of humans and mountains—or to put it another way, over what an ancient text by Dōgen means—though some seem sure that they know about the striking similarity between them. Certainly there is a dynamic among literature,

walking, and mountains, stretching from time immemorial
throughout eastern and western literature. Some of this literature is down to Earth in essays by Henry Thoreau, Gary
Snyder, or Rebecca Solnit, and some not so much.[3] None of
these texts help much in the field because we all must own
and name our own gait.

Certainly everyone who walks must be afoot. Naming this
behavior is another matter. The etymology of walking has
somehow amalgamated sources suggestive of turning or rolling, pressing or kneading; we speak of walking when we escort
another, exercise a dog, move a heavy object, or walk off an in-
jury. "Walk this way," Groucho Marx says. To speak of any person's way of walking may be to critique a way of life: To speak
of the walking manners of species is to enter an evolutionary
debate. To speak of one's own walking is to engage in some kind
of introspection—or ought to be.

Though it should to be easy to figure out what one means
when one says "I am going for a walk," one is never footloose
and fancy-free. You could call a mountain walk a scramble,
suggesting an eager, rude clambering, a contest that involves
struggling with obstacles. Or you might speak of rambles, like
night wanderings, sometimes across private property, by those
who are extravagant. Or speak of travels more gently: to amble.
When engaged in mountain walking, sometimes I amble,
sometimes I scramble, sometimes I ramble. This is more than
playing with diction or rhyme.

According to various sources, walking in mountains is
called hillwalking in Britain, or sometimes fellwalking in the
Lake District and the Yorkshire Dales—a fell being high, uncultivated, or marginal land. Mountain walking can sometimes
involve scrambling. Also, British people and nineteenth-
century Americans speak of rambling. Rambles and scrambles.
Mountain walking is a distinctly nineteenth-century activity,

recommended as a health benefit; it requires, according to those who recommend it, a bit of "know how."

According to Leslie Stephen, British writer, mountaineer, and father of Virginia Woolf, "whilst all good and wise men necessarily love the mountains, those love them best who have wandered longest in their recesses, and have most endangered their own lives and those of their guides in the attempt to open out routes amongst them."[4] There's not much chance of me endangering my "guides": They are all established literary figures these days.

People who are spoken of as keen or untiring mountain walkers aspire to move across the mountains, but for what? To open out routes? To obtain knowledge, a feeling of freedom, a sense of perspicacity, or just for the exercise? On what does the mountain walker focus, on the rock or on his own motion? Surely everyone gets tired eventually.

In a poem many read in college, "Eye and Tooth" by Robert Lowell, the narrator exclaims, "I am tired. Everyone's tired of my turmoil."[5] To walk might help calm such agitation, direct it outward, or lose it. I am at a loss about this. The psychologists speak of simple steps you can use to calm turmoil: breathing deeply from your diaphragm, repeating a mantra. Valerie and I take to the rock as if it were a mantra, knowing that danger is there, the risk of a long fast fall. One does not want to lose one's self into the all and everything. As Ishmael says, you could plunge right into annihilation. "Heed it well, ye Pantheists!"[6]

There are slower falls. Remember Ralph Waldo Emerson who, before he was seventy years old, started having memory problems and suffered from aphasia. According to Emersonian lore, by the end of his seventh decade he forgot his own name at times. Yet he remained ambulatory. When asked how he felt, he responded, "Quite well; I have lost my mental faculties, but am perfectly well."[7] The loss happens within us, perhaps, and being as ephemeral as ourselves, does not matter in the world.

In the mountains as in life, it is all up and down. With age, we have discovered that ascent is easier on the body than descent. In case you think there is only one way down, consider the following suggestions from Walter Benjamin and Gary Snyder. For Walter Benjamin, descent from a mountain is shattering (he uses the word *Erschütterung*, which suggests shattering or concussion, agitation, vibration, shock); these steps "shatter his entire body." Yet he also writes, "the partition walls inside him collapse, and he pushes on through the rubble of the moment as if in a dream. Who knows whether it is his thoughts that shatter him, or the roughness of the way? His body has become a kaleidoscope that at each step presents him with ever-changing figures of the truth."[8]

On those sometimes steep piles of rocks that accumulate below cliffs, chutes, and slopes, Gary Snyder's more agile talus-hopper performs something like "irregular dancing." Snyder writes, "The breath and eye are always following this uneven rhythm," and thus he claims that "the body-mind is so at one with this rough world that it makes these moves effortlessly once it has had a bit of practice. The mountain keeps up with the mountain."[9]

I am neither as agile as Snyder's idealized talus-hopper nor as daunted as Benjamin on descent. In matters of feet and rock I wish to reconcile weak flesh with the hard surfaces on which I scramble, so that the mind-body is at one with this rough world, as Snyder intones. I have always considered myself reasonably agile in the mountains, but descending as Snyder describes seems beyond me. Sooner or later, anyone who descends talus so aggressively is likely to lose the rhythm and get into trouble. Consequently I consider—have always considered—my walking imperfect and incomplete. I have not achieved an ideal; I cannot correct my gait; nowhere is this more obvious than when descending.

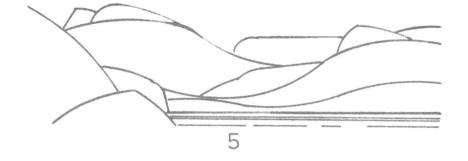

5

Glacial Polish

What makes these rocks shine?

But when they come to these pavements,
they go down on their knees and rub their hands
admiringly on the glistening surface,
and try hard to account for its
mysterious smoothness and brightness.

JOHN MUIR[1]

ANYONE WHO COMES to Tuolumne Meadows is arrested by surfaces, impressive in their reach and finish.

Six years before Muir arrived here, Josiah Dwight Whitney, head of the California Geological Survey, went on an excursion where he found "the finest mountain view in the United States" from Mount Dana. "Language can't do justice to its grandeur," he wrote. What's more, in "this great glacier region," he found the valleys "most superbly polished and grooved by glaciers," so that the "beauty of the polish on the rocks, covering hundreds of square miles of surface, is something which must be seen to be appreciated." According to him, even Yosemite Valley "did not seem so great after we had camped for a week at an elevation of nearly 10,000!"[2] Indeed, Whitney's California Geological Survey gave the name to Tuolumne Meadows.[3]

This granite of Yosemite has been inscribed by the elements and written upon repeatedly, according to Muir, so that it is like a palimpsest. Also, some features or surfaces of rocks have been erased by the elements, especially by ice. Nobody who comes to Tuolumne Meadows can fail to be impressed with the shining rock. What is this surface and how did it occur? What does it reveal? People come here from all over the world to admire the glacial polish. How or why does it satisfy some need?

In 1871, when John Muir wrote his first article about Yosemite's glaciers, his key piece of evidence was glacial polish.[4] Glacial polish can be described simply enough, since a "hallmark of glaciated landscapes is the smooth, glossy bedrock surface formed under glaciers," as Shalev Siman-Tov of UC Santa Cruz, Yosemite's present geologist Greg Stock, and other co-authors write. They examined surfaces along a fifteen-mile segment of glacial pathway from Mount Lyell down to Daff Dome recently because glacial polish "potentially holds information about subglacial conditions and processes." These authors find it technically interesting "because it forms a resistant surface that protects landscapes against postglacial weathering."[5] Valerie and I have a more enthusiastic interest.

Glacial polish on hard granitic rocks is remarkably persistent and may last up to fifty million years in certain places, though probably only a few thousand years in Yosemite. Such persistence seems to demonstrate that rock is not ephemeral and that the marks of time are also imperfect. The permanence of granitic rocks in Yosemite is revealed where it has been polished in many places to a bright sheen. This mirror sharpness has its larger and more lasting mythos as bare naked rock.

For instance, what we now call Tenaya Lake was once under many thousands of feet of moving ice. According to Muir, Indians referred to this as the "Lake of Shining Rocks." A few decades later, François E. Matthes thought "highly appropriate . . . the old Indian name for the lake—Py-we-ack, meaning the 'water of shining rocks,'" and he thought the region notable for "massive and almost wholly bare granite."[6] The career of Matthes (1874–1948) includes both rigorous professional and elegant popular writing on the geology, glaciology, and topography of Yosemite. With the exception of Muir, he remains the most influential narrator of Yosemite's geological history. We will hear much more about his studies of Yosemite's glaciology and topography.

Something more than abrasion happened under the glaciers to create these impressive expanses of gleaming granite, and there is good evidence for the theory that a coating on the rock accounts for its persistent gloss. Clearly the surfaces have been abraded and made smooth, but abrasion may also be "simultaneously producing the wear products that become the construction material for the coating layer," perhaps made of rock flour paste and silica gel.[7]

Glacial polish is rarely a perfectly smooth finish, and so one can learn a great deal from the imperfections found in it. Scratches and grooves attest to the direction of glaciers, but the surface of the rock is also laid bare and smoothed, revealing imperfections in the rock itself, variations in texture, intrusions of newer materials, and sometimes remnants of embedded material that the granite has intruded upon. The effect is that you feel like you are looking into the rock.

Also, these smooth slabs of rock occur where glaciers have had their greatest effect, typically on broad expanses, wide open slopes from which a walker can see a long way in the bright sunshine. Where the glacial polish wears off, rock reveals its true nature and shapes of crystals appear. Dikes, where sheets of resistant intrusive rock filled fractures, stand out and sometimes create webs of lines.

As Matthes wrote metaphorically, these dikes "are the more conspicuous because of the contrast between their whiteness and the somber tones of the basic rocks . . . On the curving back of Half Dome, for instance, especially in a grazing light— that is a light striking the surface at a very slight angle—they appear like the branching vein on the back of a man's hand."[8]

Rock begins to reveal myriad colors: pink, gray, white, black. Lichens in cracks are busy doing their own little destructions, as are the roots of plants. Rock is never featureless. Granite is not gray, but only appears that way from a distance. Distance. Gray ghosts. Cracks, crystals, edges, dikes: Granite is full of almost symmetrical features.

One recognizes aplite easily on surfaces of granite slopes and cliffs, as a light-colored, fine-grained, smooth intrusion into the larger mass of granite, composed mainly of chunky feldspar and quartz. The name comes from a Greek word for "simple," through German, to indicate aplite's uniformity of texture and simplicity of structure. Look at Cathedral Peak Granodiorite, cut by snaky white aplite lines, most only a few inches thick.

Aplite dikes stand out as light-colored bands in almost all granite, some fine as porcelain and some medium grained, smooth because "equigranular." These dikes must have been injected into granodiorite at a late stage of crystallization when no dark minerals remained in the magma. Most geologists think aplites crystalize from the ultimate residual melt only after most of the granite's crystallization is completed. Aplites are rich in quartz and alkali feldspar and sometimes muscovite. One notices how aplite dikes retain their integrity after adjacent granodiorite has lost it. Obviously, these dikes resist weathering better than granodiorite. They stand out in bold relief.

We use these dikes for climbing upon rocks. There are many routes named for dikes—Snake Dikes, Spiral Dikes. Smooth and pleasing because they weather more slowly than the surrounding rock, one can hold onto them or find footholds upon them, but they are slippery too.

These dikes reveal fractures within plutons at the same time as they cement the rock. These dikes reveal change and yet provide stability. They are not like living things, though we name them as if they were. Trees fall and rot. Those we love die. Meadows dry and erode. The inanimate lasts longer than us, but still these insolent surfaces indicate their history. Rock, especially polished rock, remains as a kind riddle written in braille.

6

Signs of
Exfoliation and Change

Granite comes apart! Fissures near and far.

That this may be a sign among you,
that when your children ask their fathers
in time to come, saying,
What mean ye by these stones?

JOSHUA 4:6

CLIMBERS ARE TAUGHT to yell the warning "Rock!" when a piece of the mountain is dislodged. In the year I joined the Sierra Club, 1959, Don Goodrich was killed that June when he dislodged a loose block on the southwest face of Mount Conness. A plaque at the base of the route now reads:

DONALD Q. GOODRICH
BORN–SALINAS, CALIF.
6 APRIL 1932
DIED–MT. CONNESS
13 JUNE 1959
PLACED HERE
BY HIS MANY FRIENDS

Later that summer I was led by a ranger naturalist up the easy route to that peak, and there was much discussion about the folly of technical rock climbing by, as one naturalist put it, "hammer-headed piton-pounders." I do not believe I was in Tuolumne Meadows when Goodrich pulled off that block, but I imagined that I had been. His accident was on everyone's mind that summer.

Goodrich was a twenty-seven-year-old graduate student at UC Berkeley. My father was appalled that young people should waste their lives climbing dangerous mountains. A few years later, he insisted that I read an article in *The Nation* by David Cort, "Mountaineers: Dilettantes of Suicide."[1] It was already too late to turn back. I had read Maurice Herzog's *Annapurna* and could recite Herzog's arguments about the value of such dangerous undertakings. I was already indoctrinated. Tuolumne Meadows started me on a path that led to more of the same.

I create a paradox when I put my trust in rock, knowing that these seemingly massive and featureless surfaces are always coming apart, like reality and desire. As Greg Stock points out, "Yosemite Valley has more documented rock falls than any other comparable-sized area," and with so many people pouring into the Valley, rock becomes a significant hazard. Stock is in the business of risk management, but he has a different notion of risk from my own.[2]

Certainly, if you put enough people in Yosemite Valley, at all times and in all seasons, someone will get crushed by rockfall; this continues to happen periodically. Filling Yosemite Valley to the brim guarantees that risk management will become a number-one priority—both an ongoing research project and ultimately an impossibility.

Most recently, Stock and a co-author have been studying what they call "thermally induced rockfall," measuring the daily expansion of cracks in exfoliating granite. Not surprisingly, they claim that rockfall is more likely during the warmest

months at the warmest times of day. As they put it, "seemingly
static bedrock landscapes are, in fact, quite dynamic," and huge
sheets of rock deform daily in and out of cliff faces. This leads
to the "instability of sheeted cliffs" and "highlights a potential
positive feedback loop in promoting detachment of exfoliation
sheets."[3] Will more climbing create more rockfall? Sometimes.
But there are larger forces at work here. Climbers have known
this for decades.

How well is the world holding together? One looks for
signs. After the Tioga Road (Highway 120) was rebuilt in the
years between 1957 and 1961, the National Park Service in-
stalled substantial redwood signs pointing out various features to hurrying motorists. Two of my favorites, sequenced in
fresh scars from the road cut above Yosemite Creek, included
one that said "EXFOLIATING GRANITE," and one that said
"THIS IS A GLACIAL MORAINE." Much later, when these
signs fell into disuse, they moldered behind a maintenance
building in Tuolumne Meadows that had once been a CCC
Mess Hall, later became a residence for the first winter rangers,
then was used as the center for climbing guides where Valerie
and I lived, and now houses the visitor's center. I always cov-
eted those signs, but did not have the means to carry them
away. Not having a glacial moraine or exfoliating granite indoors, researchers go outside to examine the structural coher-
ence of granitic objects.

A glacial cirque at Little Shuteye Pass, just south of Yosemite
National Park, is favored for views and photos of exfoliation
precisely because one can drive to it. Here, as elsewhere, this
phenomenon occurs in rocks with relatively homogeneous
structure and is hastened by repeated daily heating and cool-
ing. These expansions and contractions either liberate or create stress in rock to produce radial and concentric cracks so
that outer layers eventually peel off—exfoliate like an onion,

like arched or whorled fragments of weathered wood, broken at their grain.

Mind you, granite is never entirely homogeneous but because of its history is filled with pockets and protuberances, most of them buried within but many appearing on its surfaces. Granite is not cosmetically perfect, and that is part of what makes it so unendingly interesting so that wherever you go it is dependably consistent while never entirely the same. To put this differently, granite is never an abstract substance and continues to change its face as its surfaces are subjected to the elements. This is why it is possible to climb upon it.

Seeking this place, Shuteye Pass, the geologist J. David Rogers examines its dynamic and observes the "most poignant exposure I've ever encountered." He revels in "the profusion of exfoliation jointing at this location in the Mount Givens granodiorite, the strongest rock we ever tested at Berkeley" and probably the strongest rock in California. Of radial and tangential stresses developed beneath an exposed face, he explains that rock free to expand and contract will develop no stress, but when it is "constrained between two systematic joints, significant stresses can result." The very strength of some rock produces "the closest sheet joint spacings, because brittle rocks have a low strain tolerance," he writes—and then he turns personal: "This explained the countless observations I had made as a rock climber during the previous decade."[4]

In Rogers's sense, exfoliation reveals the inner structure of granitic forms, the structure below the structure one sees or touches. Yet there is something both majestic and essentially sad about exfoliation, especially here by this dirt road, and maybe even on the monumental shoulder of Half Dome. Exfoliation literally means the stripping of leaves in the fall—a process geology borrows by analogy. Consequently, the process is imbued with an elegiac tone, classically expressed by

Gerard Manley Hopkins's poetic question, "Márgarét, áre you gríeving / Over Goldengrove unleaving?" in the poem "Spring and Fall"—and in his answer: "It ís the blight man was born for, / It is Margaret you mourn for."[5]

Exfoliation of granite sometimes produces striking vertical fissures and cracks that seem to provide ideal opportunities for elegant and difficult climbing. Getting around on less steep but more exfoliated granite can be awkward. Particularly, attempting to ascend these convex inverted stairways can foster some sense of uncertainty and clumsiness. On such everyday patterns of exfoliation, on common ubiquitous granite slopes, sometimes one seeks nothing more than a way home. It is dizzying getting down the walls of Tenaya Canyon where the whole landscape seems to be peeling away below one's feet.

Under the circumstances, what is the trust I feel as I choose these footholds on seemingly massive but also expanding surfaces of rock? Am I trying to get back to the bottom of things by ascending any of these many domes? I rely on the veracity and integrity of these ripples of ice-scoured granite; I feel confident, sure of their solidity, of my grounding. Which leads to a certain comfort, or consolation, as sun glints off the striations on these glacially sculpted slabs.

A climber has to believe that rock is faithful to its own origins and that is why it exfoliates. You might call it fidelity. To climb confidently, I must believe in granite—or even sandstone and sometimes limestone. I also believe that a world of naked rock is best approached in silence, without crowds. I possess, in other words, something of the aesthetic of the traditional romantic depictions of places like Yosemite, or the dark-skyed aesthetic made so very popular by Ansel Adams. I investigate it to its ground.

Obviously, this return to rock enacts a desire for permanence. In my wandering here, I desire to transform geological ground into bedrock for personal and even institutional trust—or so I say. Permanence validates memory. Granite is for me a metaphor for memory. I care that these walks upon this ground will be for others, as they are for me today, satisfactory reminders about something that matters. According to Arkady Renko, a character in Martin Cruz Smith's *Polar Star*, who attributes this wisdom darkly to Stalin, "Happiness is the maximum agreement of reality and desire."[6] I learned this motto early, in slightly different form, as expressed by Friedrich Engels: "Freedom is the recognition of necessity." As a friend puts it, this alignment of reality and desire, freedom and necessity is both violent and idealistic, impossible and mandatory.

Clichés about changeless rocks abound. Rock solid. Rock bottom. Rock-ribbed. Rock and roll. Between a rock and a hard place. I suppose these are clichés because of the truth they express and that we know: Rock will not fit in your pocket; rock is multifaceted and fundamental. But knowledge is not the same as experience. I am devoted to the experience of rock. I do not wish to believe I am an ambulatory cliché, but maybe I am when I find myself repeating a mantra while on the move:

> Sometimes there's a change in the ocean
> Sometimes there's a change in the sea
> Sometimes there's a change in my own true love
> But there'll never be a change in me.[7]

One day, near the end of winter, while laboring up a snowy path or road, a boulder appears in front of me, as large as tomorrow. It wasn't there yesterday.

Exfoliation is hardly a new discovery. Near the turn of the nineteenth century, Grove Karl Gilbert noticed this phenomenon in Yosemite.[8] His theory remains my favorite of several explanations. After overlying strata are removed, the previously compressed and deeply buried rock begins to expand and a resulting tensile stress fractures the surface, creating layers parallel to the ground. In his *Geologic History of Yosemite Valley* (1930), François Matthes refers many times to "exfoliation shells." This geological term is rooted in a double metaphor, probably acquired by geology in the early nineteenth century.

Because *exfoliation* refers etymologically to a stripping of leaves—or human skin, or a rusty bolt, or Yosemite's Half Dome—the term itself is a second-order metaphor when used geologically. This process, sometimes but not accurately discussed as "sheet structure," is probably driven by deep forces internal to batholiths, those large intrusions of granite rooted deep in the Earth's crust (as you see, more metaphor!). Exfoliation, one might say, renews the surface of rock by opening up a fresh shape underneath.[9]

Grove Karl Gilbert's biographer, Stephen J. Pyne, notes that Gilbert proposed "various mechanisms for generating convex hilltops."[10] He typically speaks of geological processes as the hard, dry work of physics and his language certainly takes the poetry of plants out of the dynamics of granite, inserting instead a more austere poetry of engines, pistons, and machines, which I sometimes adopt.

Some people might imagine that this eternal dynamic of uncovering allows rocky forms to beautify themselves, but that is a silliness. Exfoliation along sheeting joints also makes rocks dangerous. That old engraved redwood highway sign perched above a road cut near Tuolumne Meadows might have said, "Beware! Exfoliating Granite!" Clearly there is some confusion or conflict between the geological processes of Yosemite and the safety of the visitors. The very processes that bring visitors also put them at risk.

We had best watch our footing, for this solid Earth is more unstable than it seems. My touchiness about this paradox is obvious. An illusion I hold dear, the basic premise of most of my years, has been that these variegated slabs are stable and very long-lived if not eternal—like the federally reserved regions in which they reside. I climb upon these surfaces as if they were eternal. That is what trust means. Well, not exactly. I do not grab a thin flake on steep rock without inspecting it. They are not entirely trustworthy, nor is my judgment, nor are the institutions that protect them.

When I used to teach composition to freshmen, I found that my students made a frequent mistake, writing "take it for granite" when they meant "take it for granted." Perhaps this is precisely my error: to "take it for granite." What we take for granted is not necessarily given.

Nevertheless, I have been running and walking below and climbing upon these rocks for fifty years. Despite the fact that many routes I climbed have sloughed off the surfaces of cliffs, slopes, and domes that permitted them, I have come away unscathed. I have never worn a helmet while climbing or scrambling or mountain-walking on Yosemite granite. So perhaps the situation is not as bad as the risk managers suppose, or else I have been lucky. For one thing, there are so many documented landslides and rockfalls in Yosemite Valley precisely because people have scrutinized these steep walls so painstakingly. All mountains experience wastage, as Victorian mountaineers noted. The mountains are always coming down to us.

If things were so impermanent, how could I find the wonderful surfaces of glacially polished rock, surfaces that are tens of thousands of years old, still shining in the sunlight? Or the lovely aprons of rock on which water slides, or the great expanses of crystalline rock on alpine peaks? Why does the rock glisten; why is the water so clear? Why are the shapes so consistently appealing, as if consciously sculpted? These are not questions of physics. If I have to believe something, I will continue to believe in rock.

So why is it that I don't much like being in the wind these days? I don't think it used to bother me so much. I enjoy observing changes in the world less and less and do not welcome the presaging signs of change. It is not just the impermanence of rock that worries me—it is the impending impermanence of everything, including myself. In Joseph Heller's *Good as Gold* (1979), the protagonist Bruce Gold asserts not only that "nothing succeeds as planned" and "every change is for the worse," but also that "we are not a society, or we are not worth our salt." He is alluding to Matthew 5:13: "Ye are the salt of the Earth: but if the salt have lost his savour, wherewith shall it be salted? it is thenceforth good for nothing, but to be cast out, and to be trodden under foot of men." I sometimes feel like Gold. What are we worth?

I can only recover or recall certain memories, marks of successful changes, though not necessarily as planned. Perhaps this place embodies the most important changes in my life and I survive them.

Valerie and I are not the first people who wanted to live permanently in Tuolumne Meadows. Back in those days, people like the father of my historian colleague Robert Righter camped in the Meadows for whole summers. The old Tioga Road, originally a mining road, offered a slow and difficult drive on a rough one-way lane, a journey that sifted out casual tourists in a hurry. Sometimes Valerie and I find ourselves among the old unsuccessful gold mines scattered all over the higher passes near Tuolumne Meadows, monuments to unfounded beliefs, their structures weathering in the wind, their shafts filling with water and gravel.

But between 1957 and 1961, the Tioga Road was widened and realigned, and the new road allowed fast and easy access to Tuolumne Meadows. It became a highway. People traveled it just to drive from east to west and vice versa. A great deal changed and we came with that road. I became a climbing guide and Valerie became a ranger. We have been complicit in those changes here, being brought into it at a key moment, named Mission 66 by the Park Service, when the Tioga Road was reengineered and access to the high country was made so much easier. Since then, the infrastructure of Yosemite has undergone many significant alterations. The Sierra changes too and will change more rapidly now, in ways we can barely imagine and won't live to see.

Nevertheless there are certain places that do not so much remind me of the past as make me feel like I am situated in an eternal present. This is no doubt an illusion that I can best hold onto when on the granite peaks and domes surrounding Tuolumne Meadows. The enigma of change and the tricks people use to reveal it, such as repeat photography, seem pointless to me now. One must witness what happens day by day and year by year to experience and decide whether essentials change. This is not a matter of imagery.

For those aficionados of the granitic forms of Tuolumne Meadows the idea of repeat photography seems nearly redundant because this activity is largely meant to reveal a history of photographic choices for admiring the forms of large landmarks.[11] The same rocks seen from exactly the same places. Though these rocks have changed, such changes are mostly beyond the scope of the history of photography. Repeat photography on a different scale might reveal changes known to climbers: the disappearance of "Psyche Flake" on Half Dome, the recent great rockfalls on the east edge of El Capitan, the scouring of the Glacier Point Apron by rockfall. These have not been a focus for repeat photography. A history of photographs for Yosemite's glaciers might be another matter, but we don't need photographs to tell us what has happened and is happening to the climate of Yosemite.

In my more exuberant moments—though they occur less frequently now—I don't care what wonderful granite forms people used to have, but only what domes I can ascend right now and maybe, if I am thinking really far ahead, what these rocks will be like next spring when the snow melts and the music of water begins again.

Consequently Tuolumne Meadows presents a microcosm of my desire for stability and permanence and my apprehension about instability and change, my ambivalence about the trajectory of time. As I witness changes in this natural and cultural landscape, I worry about changes in myself; I fear changes in the institution of Yosemite National Park and in the dedicated wilderness that advocates cobbled together across the High Sierra, protecting places that I would prefer to imagine as permanent. These institutions matter to me because they seemed to have been created according to a doctrine that I learned young and have always desired to inculcate in others. These ideals are an essential groundwork for community, such as I have experienced it.

No Earthquake can change the grounding of the Sierra, nor will drought denude it of its glory—did I finally borrow Muir's term, glory?—while it still stands. The way the mountains play with the weather remains impressive, and one expects many of these sets of patterns to recur in an ever-changing future.

Grace on Granite

Perceiving a granite landscape. Why we all like rocks.

No-one loves rock, yet we are here.

GARY SNYDER, "Paiute Creek"[1]

Look for foundations of sea-worn granite,
my fingers had the art
To make stone love stone, you will find some remnant.

ROBINSON JEFFERS, "Tor House"[2]

I touched the stones.
I liked to place my hands on the cold granite.
The stones exuded a calm that didn't exist in people …
Stone sculptures calmed me.

VLADIMIR SOROKIN, *Ice Trilogy*[3]

WALKING AND GRANITE: I cannot think about one without invoking the other. No one can know granite, at least not the granite of Yosemite, without getting right up on it—cannot know it well without a great deal of physical contact. Granite cannot be known by eyes alone: It must be known by feel, close up, with hands and feet and more, by lying upon it, sliding on it, sitting on it, smelling and even tasting it. All children know this.

As the literary critic J. Hillis Miller once joked, "Grund in Kant has nothing to do with the ground Kant walked across every day in Königsburg to get from his house to the university. But is this really so?"[4] Only going to ground, as Miller argued, will suffice: One must reach down to the foundation for belief, action, or argument, to fundamental logical conditions, to metaphysical causes with claims about the "true principles of reason."

To make a more than academic distinction: There is stone and there is rock. Stone is a material humans shape, a resistant medium. Jeffers writes in "Continent's End" that life "envies hardness, the / insolent quietness of stone," and though I do envy the hardness of stone, I'm not entirely sure what he means.[5] Writers on geology suffer over a distinction between rock and stone.[6] As built by human minds and hands into towers, walls, fences, chimneys, roofs, castles, roads, trails, sculptures, tools, jewelry—and perhaps gravel pits as Lucy Lippard, a theorist of conceptual art, argues—stone reveals the human signature.[7] Rock humans let lie, though certainly not without inscriptions. Writing on rock, as in pictograph and petroglyph, and writing with stone are different acts. Consider the tombstone, quarried from granite, shaped, transported, engraved, and replanted. Is it no longer rock but stone—or both?

You could love stone because of what you can make *with* it; you could love rock because of what you can make *of* it, in memory and actuality. You can love yourself too. Humanists might revere the harmony between body and mind in works of stone: What's to love but our own ideas, memories, and constructs of the world? One thing's for sure: Neither stone nor rock will love you.

Nevertheless, some prefer uninscribed rock for a kind of contact with the world and come to these regions of granite to luxuriate in great waves or heaves or storms of rock. These forceful patterns are made of granites that seem in motion but also seem eternally still. Call out the rock, as Snyder would have it: Here we are. In this sense, some people still read John Muir because he articulated a central human desire: to attend to graceful rock. A desire for a world that seems elegant, finished, refined, with balance, form, style, and symmetry.

I believe there *is* something one might call grace, born out of features of this cold rock, as from the Latin *gratia* for favor, esteem, regard, or good will, gratitude. By definition, grace comes from unmerited favor and selflessness. But this cannot be true. One can only be favored by cold rock if one chooses to reshape the movement of the human body to meet this realm. There is this paradox—that grace is given and yet must be earned. I learned this lesson repeatedly on this granite. Grace goes beyond the agility of bodies. Grace offers permission—a privilege or concession that cannot be claimed as a right. One climbs by grace, but of what? To speak of grace, I enter a difficult terrain that seethes with religious ideas and doctrines. I will do it nevertheless. Everyone lives by illusions.

After my apprenticeship with the rangers, I learned how to climb mountains and how to get around in a granite landscape by reading John Muir. It took some time, as I followed his and other examples on various peaks and in canyons of Tenaya Creek and the Tuolumne River.

As it happened, I was on Cathedral Peak on the centennial of John Muir's ascent of September 7, 1869. In more than one sense, I carried his *First Summer in the Sierra* with me. What, I wondered, would one say if Muir had invented his story of climbing Cathedral Peak? Surely his expression for this peak— "a temple displaying Nature's best masonry and sermons in stones"—is a metaphor any modern person has a hard time swallowing: this wild-eyed, half-blind Scotsman pretending this was the first time he was in church in California! Perhaps his narrative is meant to give symmetry to his extended essay about that First Summer—assuming, of course that he did indeed ascend the exposed last pitch to the very summit. What Cathedral Peak's rock holds within itself certainly fascinated him, "sparkling with crystals—feldspar, quartz, hornblende, mica, tourmaline."[8] First Summers reveal a human desire for an awakening within.

For Muir and his followers, forms like Cathedral Peak invite and epitomize a large set of desires. The primary desire is also to belong—to be sufficiently adapted to this place, in contact and conversation with its landforms, that you feel comfortable and attuned while moving upon them. In a granite region like this, you desire and sometimes discover abilities of your own body. This is what climbers believe. Historians, of course, have shown that these largely aesthetic qualities are, as they say, social constructs, revealing the perceivers and their cultural dispositions. Why else would anyone be carrying Muir's text?

People feel—or hope to feel—ease or poise in such places; perhaps they are biologically programmed for this, as the human ecologist Paul Shepard used to insist. They may even feel agile or dexterous. Consider these rock climbers who come to Yosemite where they seem to dance and who engage in a difficult discipline of their bodies and minds to do so. There is something about this graceful rock that makes a perceiver feel it is necessary to earn the right to abide on it by elegant moves. Grace prevents falls.

As a result, the sense of favor, goodness, benevolence, and virtue that such monumental rock as that of Yosemite provides *at certain times* borders on the religious. On the one hand, there is the suggestion that this must be earned by right action on the part of the perceiver. We study and learn practices of the wild so we will be worthy to be in it.

 On the other hand, we who live in a consumer culture know that it is possible to pick and choose, to buy our pleasures. Which is why most people go to the wilds largely during those times they can easily acquire these favored feelings. We avoid times of adversity, and being modern creatures, can do so. When storms move in, campgrounds empty: Backpackers come pouring out of the woods. We choose quiet seasons, even deciding whether we will get out of the automobile. Doing so— and who can tell us that we are morally wrong to do so—we miss the sense of the returning equipoise of the world when a storm clears or the wind stops blowing. When carefully drying wet clothes on smooth granite slabs after being soaked, one receives on one's own body the benediction of the returning sun.

 Fortunately, the mountains here are mostly gentle on the visitor, as the title of one book published by the Sierra Club suggests, but the storms of the Sierra are violent on some days too.[9] It is always a surprise to discover that there are people who do not know how to accommodate themselves to changes in the mountains, who do not even know how to step on wet rock. For instance, do not trust your footing in the rain on rock where water has run in the spring. You will slip. It is a disappointment to meet people who do not know that grace must be earned. Climbers speak of easy or difficult moves and practice them on boulders, over and over. All of us may ask explicitly for benediction or even blessing, at no time more than after a lost sense of ease on rock. But these must be learned and earned.

 Like many others, I have damaged myself by venturing too far under conditions unsuitable to my mental and physical strength. A decade after I heard the news about Don Goodrich, I found myself involved in rescues and sometimes in recoveries

of bodies in Yosemite. I have retrieved damaged and sometimes lifeless younger people and older ones, too, who ven-
tured beyond their abilities. What solace for those who are
injured? There is some line between damage and inconve-
nience, and there is no substitute for skill and wisdom: The
visitor who hopes for agility must learn this.

Before people learned to make stone love stone, I would
answer, rock loved itself. This place may seem created in
symmetry and restful contemplation because perceivers
seek something more in themselves and, though often disappointed, are sometimes rewarded. Something abides inside a
mountain, and we imagine it is there within solid rock.

Now, as I move onto granite with Valerie, what do I seek? Some
might be satisfied with knowledge of the geomorphology of
rock, but I also cannot help exploring a geomythology of granite—to dream of it in traditional ways, with images that come
through gates of ivory or gates of horn. I have slept on more
than one granite ledge in Yosemite. I have not always slept well.

Yosemite granite has always been part of our dreams. I
don't care anymore whether this is only a granite of our imagination, with its subtle modulations and its overall regularity.
On glaciated granite we always seem to know where to go.
There are geological reasons for this, but these reasons do not
suffice to account for the experience. Maybe when roaming on
granite domes, we seek the hearts of these many plutons. This
is, of course, an impossibility. Granite has no heart.

More to the point, perhaps, many respectable people don't
know how to speak of their own hearts. *Alexithymia* is a clin-
ical term often used to describe rock climbers. It means, literally, a lack of words, but more generally an inability to describe
emotions within oneself. As I have read, those who suffer from

this malady fail to have a "full emotional life," or to put it another way, lack emotional intelligence. I myself have few and insufficient words for my emotions and partake of this malady or quality owned by some who inhabit "high-risk domains." The emotions involved in rock climbing and mountaineering, like fear, are salient and easily identifiable as outcrops.

Imagine a person who finds it difficult to identify feelings or who confuses feelings and bodily sensations; one who has difficulty articulating these, who suffers from a scarcity of fantasies, and who is driven by stimulus to an externally oriented cognitive style.[10] An objective correlative for this psychic situation might be granite.

Not finding the arguments of psychologists particularly convincing, one must own them and ask: "What is being risked exactly by those who have commerce with hard rock that can be imagined as more valuable than life itself?" Shall we understand that people like me take risks because they cannot articulate their emotions? Do some go to granite, to insolent indurate granite—go to ground—because of a wish to escape the chaos of emotions? I would rather say something closer to what T. S. Eliot had in mind when he wrote, "Poetry is not a turning loose of emotion, but an escape from emotion; it is not the expression of personality, but an escape from personality. But, of course, only those who have personality and emotions know what it means to want to escape from these things."[11]

It is no wonder that the Sierra Nevada and Yosemite in particular are filled with what we call landmarks. The geohumanist Jared Farmer explains precisely that only as a result of human history a landmark becomes "a legible feature of the landscape where meaning is concentrated."[12] Because landmarks are constructed or created by stories, they constantly change.

Consider one moment, the story of a well-known photo-graph that established a landmark, "Monolith, the Face of Half Dome, Yosemite National Park, 1927" by Ansel Adams. As the "official" story goes,

> On an April morning in 1927, Adams undertook a dif-ficult four-thousand-foot climb through heavy snow to the granite outcropping known as the Diving Board, where he set up his 6½ × 8½-inch view camera, inserted a glass plate, and waited for the light to fall directly on the sheer granite cliff. He made one exposure with a yel-low filter. Then it occurred to him that if he used a dark red filter, both sky and cliff would register darker in the finished print than in the actual scene. He changed to the red filter, with this dramatic result. He described this episode as his first "visualization"—his attempt to express the emotional and aesthetic feelings he felt at the time he made the photograph. Adams considered it a seminal moment in his development as a photographer.[13]

The historian in me says Adams's image manipulated and stylized the light of Muir's Range of Light. Cold rock through a red filter! Literary tradition channeled through the use of a camera. By definition, all human concentration of meaning becomes a highly stylized abstraction. Consequently, this and all of his photographs reveal Adams as much as they reveal Half Domes and El Capitans, and these images participate in or create landmarking. These mechanically reproduced photographs in black and white are stories in themselves. So it was that these literary images grabbed my attention when very young and held it, beckoned me to put hands on Yosemite granite, which I have done over and over. When I entered George Kennedy's laboratory, I was already a de-voted rock climber.

The narrative that supplements Adams's image gives climbing a certain kind of authority. Galen Rowell and other photographer acquaintances of mine used, and continue to use, this argument to authorize their own images. They believe that those who climb the cliffs gain a unique and special kind of vision, achieve grace. Perhaps I also make such a claim. Perhaps not.

So now I wonder: What if there is some more intimate relation to rock than through creating landmarks or celebrating them? What if one does not wish to concentrate meaning? What if meaning is so widely dispersed that it never requires waiting for a chance to obtain spectacular views or ascend familiar routes? What if meaning passes into something available everywhere there is granite? Well, that is not quite right, because knowing a place well enough allows landmarks to proliferate. Specific ledges, cracks, bowls, even specific boulders acquire significance and sometimes names.

What does it mean or do to one to read, name, or narrate a landscape? Is there, for instance, a Rosetta Stone for the Sierra Nevada? And is that decoder to be found in indigenous narratives, folklore, pioneer journals, travelers' notes, literary works, photographs, or geological, biological, or geographical studies? Or is a reading to be found in websites, advertisements, roadside signs and exhibits, visitors centers? Can one read with one's hands and feet, as Valerie and I and many of our friends have tried to do?

In human individuals, too, meaning is concentrated. We have met plenty of interesting characters while climbing in Yosemite—and some pretty boring ones. Most of our climbing partners are gone from our lives these days, and more will be gone soon. Our generation is passing away. Other generations are climbing these rocks. More power to them. However, my narrative is not a history of climbing. We gave up our relation to granite through athletic activity long ago. Now it is a story of our most intimate relationships through rock.

When we were young, men climbed mostly with men and men climbed occasionally with women. Later, women climbed with women. Although women constituted only a small percentage of climbers in Yosemite during the years when I was active, they are now a significant force, many of them quite prominent. Valerie herself decided sometime in the 1960s that she was better suited to activities other than technical rock climbing. After a soul-searching conversation with our longtime friend and mentor Chuck Pratt who said she would only overcome her apprehensions by becoming more aggressive and leading climbs, she decided that this was not a challenge she wished to confront. Similar decisions have more relevance to geoscience than one might imagine.

In a recent article for *Progress in Human Geography*, Mark Carey, M. Jackson, Alessandro Antonello, and Jaclyn Rushing point out that manliness has been a pronounced virtue in the field of glaciology, one that seemed to make the science of "masculinist" glaciologists more credible. Nevertheless, they assert that "ice is not just ice." Discourses of manliness, heroism, and conquest have dominated the field and hindered entrance by women.[14] This is not surprising. Susan Schrepfer, for instance, has discussed the Victorian and post-Victorian predilection that reserved geology for men and relegated women to botany.[15]

But just as ice is not just ice, so, too, rock is not just rock. In 1974, one of our oldest friends wrote and published "Hands on Half Dome Quartz Monzonite," a critique of climbing with a male partner that might still apply. Anne Marie Rizzi was not happy because her experience conflicted so grievously with the (abusively shouting) perspective of her partner, who wanted her to lead faster while climbing on the northwest face of Half

Dome.[16] Our partnership has been more successful. Though for decades now we have divided our project—Valerie speaks with her drawings and paintings and I speak in print—yet Valerie's interest is not restricted to plants nor am I restricted to cold rock. Though the focus here is on rocks, we refuse to be relegated to only one aspect of our lives. Neither of us would like any reader to imagine that we do not enjoy the flowers of Tuolumne Meadows. We, too, wait every spring for the blooming of shooting stars, owl's clover, and Lemmon's paintbrush.

Valerie remains my steadfast partner, and we continue to walk, if not to climb, often alone in this crowded national park not because we seek solitude but because our itineraries take us to places others do not choose. The physical liveliness of our own bodies is leaving us, but what I call the grace of granite remains. Everyone has their own place. Ours is somewhere near the center of the Tuolumne Intrusive Suite. It is true: There are secret places known only by those who climb rocks. On the other hand, everyone has their own granite.

One need not go to a national park to seek solitude. There is no doubt an ecology of our intrusive presence—what we and others do and have done here. There is an ecology of rock climbing too, but no certain ecology of rock. It is just rock. Against all obvious reason, having climbed a good many routes in and around Tuolumne Meadows, the rock of northern Yosemite has been my passion. Now I am no longer climbing routes; my passion has modulated. It is time to contemplate rock: not what grows on it, but how it grows on one.

Unlike most but not all of our friends, we continue to return to the mountains here. When devotees of the sport can no longer climb, we have noticed, they sometimes cease to come to the mountains—not because of crowds or because of their own infirmity but because what was once their passion is now no longer possible or of value. Their interaction with rock is done. Ruth Mendenhall, my mother-in-law, is an example. When arthritis finally made hiking and climbing impossible for her, she stopped going to the mountains, even though she loved and had vast knowledge of their geology, flora, and fauna. This was no arrogance, like that of one of my partners who said years ago, "I've done Tuolumne." He lives in a large city.

During our sojourns in Tuolumne Meadows, the wilderness movement has waxed and waned. I have discussed a great deal of that history of ideas in books about John Muir and the Sierra Club.[17] The wilderness debate is not over, and we will not be done with the ideology or institutions of wilderness for a while. Meanwhile, we watch old friends who were hardline wilderness advocates follow scientists and slide into advocacy for biodiversity, and witness many of our best friends in literary and historical studies move away from their focus on biotic systems and toward social dynamics. I have learned never to write "Nature" and to rarely say "nature" when I can possibly avoid the term, and never to speak of Yosemite as wilderness. I don't want to defend the "losing side" of the wilderness debates more vociferously here. Sometimes I just want to see the end of bickering and say, "Soon rock is all we will have. We might as well get used to it."

I am also tempted to say, "There is no other life, yet there is another life." In a glaciated granite landscape we know where we are and who we are. Because we cannot abandon the mountains, we have needed a new relationship to them. So we return year after year to the same rocks in the same bare places, rocks that beckon touch and more. This is no rut. This is foundational. What we are together is not simply mediated but catalyzed by these rocks.

Whatever we do now is all about slow climbing or walking. We go slow to see where we are and know what we have been.

No longer challenged to test our bodies' limits, we no longer participate in sport here. There is nothing promiscuous about our mountain travels now. Nothing indiscriminate. We are careful in our choices, cool and restrained. This is no longer play as it once was, but something else. Though we may not be naturalists, yet we have learned from them a notion or principle of slow walking: to be observant, know where you are; know what you are observing, what you are doing and why.

The Transformation
of Things

Becoming a voice of rock.

HARD WORDS NEED to be spoken about our times. This has been coming for a while. For instance, according to Jack Kerouac, sometime in the late 1940s Allen Ginsberg "developed a tone of voice which he hoped sounded like what he called The Voice of Rock; the whole idea was to stun people into the realization of the rock." As Ginsberg himself wrote in 1948, "With voice of rock, and rock engirt, / a shadow cries out in my name;" and that shadow is "like a crystal lost in stone."[1] Ginsberg, Kerouac, Snyder: The so-called Beats shape my discourse of rock. Although popular views on the Beats suggest that they were frivolous boys, they often turned toward grim realities; like earlier American writers Emerson, Thoreau, and Whitman, they also turned to Asian texts.

What is it like to turn? To rotate around some fixed axis, to change one's nature, to exploit an opportunity. What is it like to be turned, to be bent, reshaped, or altered by some revolution? To turn up and to be turned loose. In Italian, *volta* (turn) indicates a poem's shift in the direction of thought or argument, from question to answer, from problem to solution.[2] To be turned is perhaps to be transformed.

I transform and paraphrase an account of "Zhuangzi's Butterfly Dream" into this: "Between whoever I am and the

rock, there must be some distinction!" As the *Zhuangzi* concludes, "This is called the Transformation of Things."[3] Humans
are so much more ephemeral than rock; surely there must be a
distinction between human voice, human yearning, and whatever rock intends. Touching this grainy surface of granite in
shadow, all things change, even rock itself. Rock is no dream
and has no dreams. No human voice can ever become a voice of
rock, however strong Ginsberg's yearning, but who cannot admire his desire to "stun people into the realization of the rock."

As to the turn, one finds movement everywhere, as in a
passage from John Clare (1794–1864), whose poetry, according
to his biographer, is a record of his search for a home in the
world.[4] Clare wrote, "the hairey bumble bee . . . wings out
of the wood to the sunshine that lead him to his mossy nest
lapt up in the long grass of some quiet nook—such is happiness—& to wander a pathless way thro the intricacys of woods
for a long while & at last burst unlooked for into the light of
an extensive prospect at its side & there lye & muse on the
landscape to rest ones wanderings—this is real happiness— ."[5]

Not pretending to share the perspective of either Zhuangzi's
butterfly or Clare's bee, not in these times interested in the "intricacys of woods," and no longer sure what "real happiness"
might be, I know this: There is no happiness in rock. There
cannot be. Unlike Zhuangzi or Clare, one can only rarely
imagine any creature, and especially not a butterfly, "happy
with himself and doing as he pleased."

Finally I consider the turn of a poem in Burton Watson's
1971 translation of Wang Wei's "Deer Fence":

Empty hills, no one in sight,
only the sound of someone talking;
late sunlight enters the deep wood,
shining over the green moss again.

To which a reader might respond, "That's it?"[6]

In Yosemite there is always someone talking. Now virtually everyone who visits this granite citadel is a tourist. Where did we come from? What does the granite protect? The very term *tourist* arrives in English late in the eighteenth century. Perhaps a tourist journeys for pleasure, stopping here and there like Clare's bee; perhaps a tourist is a writer. Almost by definition, tourists depart from home, carrying an intention of returning home. Some take their travels more seriously than others. Apparently, English noblemen referred to a trip undertaken for education, research, and cultural exploration as a "turn." Perhaps a tourist takes a "turn," as it was once called. As scholars note, often the underlying purpose of these travels was to acquire power and control over resources.[7] Surely the travels of Buddhist monks and pilgrims, and their writings, were also a form of tourism, or so one might suppose.

As well-seasoned tourists by the time we apprenticed ourselves to climbing granite in Yosemite, we who were learning the craft fervently believed that our commerce with those rocks constituted something of great value, something more than tourism. The rangers and proprietors of hotels disagreed. We talked about our mission volubly and often in public. Now, having been engaged with Yosemite's rock longer than as a climber of it, I remain a tourist. Nevertheless, what I feel when surrounded by granite is as close as I can get to feeling at home.

Maybe climbing is not as valuable as other activities in Yosemite—skiing, fishing, artistic and scientific endeavors, or sociological research, for instance—but climbing those granite cliffs has some value to it, and not simply as training ground for high alpinism. Hopefully one can distinguish between more and less valuable tourist activities—some more valuable on a number of grounds, and not merely that of safety. My parents thought of climbing as an extreme sport, but it was quite the opposite. We climbers came of age in Yosemite, came to adulthood through interaction with Yosemite's granite. This was never simply an athletic endeavor. Something irreversible happened to us when we took calculated risks.

Valerie and I have taken a more recent turn or radical change to slow and easy climbing. I have never been interested in flirting with death, though I certainly have been afraid and sometimes learned to control fears. Valerie found fears to be unconquerable and ceased to do technical climbing. She preferred other activities. Because of the certainty of consequences, this granite often and inescapably suggests death. It permits no mistakes—yet death is the mother of beauty according to Wallace Stevens, and conversely sleep is the sister of death according to Mohammed.

Our turn toward slow climbing does not correspond to what young climbers do in Yosemite now, which none of my contemporaries could have imagined. The past thirty years have seen an explosion of interest in extreme sport, whatever it might entail—not just unroped climbing on technically difficult routes and climbing for speed. Base jumping, aerial maneuvers on skis and snowboards, tricks on snowmobiles or motorcycles—these especially encouraged by commercial interests—take a turn past our time. These commercial games encourage young people to compete in dangerous and even reckless activities, to do fancy tricks at great speed where a mistake often results in death. Death has become the deciding factor in these extreme sports, as demographics and statistics indicate. Wonderful athletes have died or been crippled by failures. We believe that those in the mountains should have a longer view.

9

Out of Bounds

Mountain craft.

*"Well, we had maps," said Mrs. Cassady.
"But they didn't use them ... The boys didn't know where
they were going. They didn't. Not really.
They just knew that they wanted to go."*

Carolyn Cassady (2013)[1]

Even in my pre-teen years I yearned to travel the mountains by any means. Mostly I wanted to wander there, not take photographs or engage in nature study, just wanted to be out and away, to get up high in the sky and so become what I discovered was called a mountain walker. That's what I aspired to, but not without guides. I learned to use maps, then settled on a single place and a single map.

Over the last fifty years, Valerie and I pass this map back and forth almost every time we stop. The chief document we own and use, the 15-minute Tuolumne Quadrangle published in 1956 has been our main guidebook, carried for all our years in Tuolumne Meadows.[2] In a certain sense, the guiding purpose for this now-antique map has never been to keep from getting lost—although we have avoided some unnecessary steep descents and climbs by consulting it.

The real value is to remind us of the architecture of the region and sometimes to imagine it. For that reason we find the 15-minute map that depicts about 230 square miles more useful than the newer seven-and-a-half minute maps. Our maps are not pristine. On this map, like others we own, Valerie has drawn various lines, ideas on its back. On the front we have posted various events, like the fire we saw up on Mammoth Crest when we were walking below in Lyell Canyon.

When we carry a contour map we are being led by an abstraction that shapes our ways of thinking. This single sheet of folded paper gives a sufficiently broad sense of where we are, so that we can pay more attention to more immediate matters. Nevertheless, we sometimes think in terms of being on the map and off the map. Over the years, we consumed many copies of this map, taped at their folds and worn on their edges until they were in tatters.

For us, the Sierra is most certainly an architectural phenomenon. As Arthur H. Robinson writes in his classic book on cartography, "The drawing of a parallel between cartography and architecture is instructive. Each lies in the field of the practical arts; each is older than history; and each, since its beginnings, has been more or less under the control of its consumers."[3]

As contemporary consumers, we are aware that our contour map has a history. It should be no surprise to us that using this map we follow a practice shaped by Matthes, who was an early master of topographical drawing, first in the Grand Canyon and later in Yosemite. His method of mapmaking required turning multiple observations from transits into sketches that still seem remarkable for the beauty of their contour lines. As one book on cartography notes, "The simple language of the drawing allows for a focus on the landform. The steepness of the canyon—the density of lines—express the three-dimensional quality of the place without the need for further shading and texture."[4]

Despite my engagement in technical climbing, I have always been a mountain walker, committed to an agenda in mountains where there is no trail—as an aesthetic act, maybe even a craft, and something more. Everyone engages in walking, but how far does that engagement go? I would say that mountain walking in itself is not an expedient to get somewhere, or even of a way of knowing where you've been or where you've chosen to go, but has its own end as a human discipline. On the other hand (or should I say foot?), walking—even if not taken to be the real work of the world—offers one good way to enter a real world, or at least to realize a world psychically. That's how it is as one foot treads where the other doesn't. It is possible to trip if you do not juggle theory and practice, the limitations of the body and the cultural aspirations of the enterprise.

The craft of mountain walking must be learned. One needs to study how to walk this way. Like many others, I learned in a national park, where people who were once called Naturalists taught visitors to focus on ideas associated with walking—its ideology—through modes of teaching and learning. These employees are now called Interpreters; they tell visitors about trees and flowers, rocks and critters, but also teach people how to get around. There is a paradox in this. The schooling in Tuolumne Meadows, where I learned, offered a kind of digression, avoiding straight ways. This schooling began in the early 1950s. And we in turn followed this tradition when we set our son loose in the meadows of Yosemite Valley.

Carl Sharsmith (1903-1994) led peripatetic tours for decades in Tuolumne Meadows as a National Park Service ranger naturalist. In winter he was a professor of biology at San Jose State University. He was often dismissive and sometimes angry at the stupidity of those who did not revere Nature, and his outbursts remind me now of Thoreau's occasional outbursts in *Walden*.[5] I was not a great naturalist and never learned much botany from Sharsmith, but was introduced to something more important—how to behave with respect toward Yosemite's granite.

You could never be sure where Sharsmith would lead his little groups. He rarely followed trails. He was mercurial. You couldn't be sure what would make him happy or angry. Where he led diverged from the straight way, beaten path, and marked trail: His walks did not teach aspiration, but something else. All good walking, as he taught, should often be *digressive*, a *going off* or, as Sierra Club leader Joseph LeConte called it, *rambling* into the unexpected: improvisational, incomplete, and ongoing. This mental trajectory could be neither going up nor going down, and could be falling off. In any case, I followed him until I no longer required a guide or a trail.

It is best to start early, to be seduced by a morning star or a glint of sun from a scattering of crystals all aligned as they have been washed down a slope. It is to enter sidereal time, not to repeat the workday. A bit of incidental light, magnified perhaps, made extravagant by human gestures, by human syntax. Walking is a discontinuous activity, with its own unpredictable rhythm. None of us proceed in the same light, at the same speed, in the same time or same direction, nor experience the same sensations. It is impossible to take the same walk twice.

If, when now embarking on a ramble, I am foolish enough to imagine where my itinerary will lead me, what would be the point? Every moment is potentially important. As walking goes, so ought writing or spoken discourse to go—as an advent.

Yes, I am trying to get away, to get into some other state. Like most Americans, I am surrounded—literally bathed—by advertisements and news: to *advert*, turn our attention and sell us something. The adverts distract us from adventures, from *advents*, happenings in the present. Out here, one might hope to be going off on a modest adventure appropriate to one's age and condition, to little diversions from the path, small rebellions in insignificant counties.

Most walks, but not all, contain some advent, some happening. These might come upon one in the middle of things, unexpected and unframed, out of context and isolate. These advents cannot be reached through desire alone or by calculation. Climbers speak of the most challenging point as the *crux*. Walks, too, may include a planned *crux*, a difficulty that must be passed and understood. And yet no accurate report should fix them in neat and ordered structures, as if they were composed or preserved as part of some catalogued collection. The best representation of our walks, especially in Tuolumne Meadows, would be a set of incomplete rough drafts of memory and desire.

Consequently, our excursions do not have a fixed logic of beginnings-middles-ends, thesis-antithesis-synthesis, or major premise-minor premise-conclusion. They are, as the term *excursion* suggests, openings and deviations. They don't resolve themselves into a plan to follow, remember, or write about later, except as parts of portents or dreams. There is no satisfying conclusion because we are not dead yet.

We are past seventy years old. Our walks are mostly not physically difficult; except in a few experiments, they rarely require athletic prowess, though we admire athletes. These walks, these goings-off, these experiments on two feet are about some other difficulty than those that can be solved with training regimens or orthotics.

We are sometimes painfully aware that what we do in a region like Tuolumne Meadows constitutes diversions, amusements, entertainments—not an economic activity. We have learned to call this sort of activity *recreation* because it is more than an entertainment. If we are interested in recreation, then we ought to see how we re-create ourselves when we go for or "take" a walk. As modern persons, we drive to the trailhead, or drive and then take a shuttle bus. Like others, we consciously make these activities essential, even though we need not. But what is changed by our days? Heaven knows that most people drive right by the very places we choose to enter. They do not need to be going off into these places as we do. And our walking, the style that shapes an aesthetic act for us, does not follow the dictates of those from whom we have learned. My own ways are slightly different from those of my teachers or those of Valerie's teachers.

Sharsmith was only one of a set of naturalists I followed while in Tuolumne Meadows. These, as Valerie points out, were themselves a peculiar assortment. I now realize that I had to be taught first by civil servants. We understand this as a function of economic class. The father of Bob Marshall, founder of The Wilderness Society, hired guides for his son. My father threw me into the arms of our government. Though known as ranger naturalists, most of them had "real jobs" in the cities as public school teachers at high schools and colleges. I followed the same profession.

Something further. At the exact moment the Sierra Club ceased to be an elite group, I was encouraged to join, and a number of these people became my mentors, as they had been for Valerie. They were all to some extent naturalists, but few of them knew much about biology. Nor were they philosophical naturalists. They did believe that nature would make them whole—though I do not, because I do not find any cosmic meaning in the outdoors.

Later many friends and acquaintances helped me along. This group included Valerie and her parents, Ruth and John Mendenhall. The history of my travels here has become a miniature history of my own social and intellectual mobility, for which I am eternally grateful. All these people believed something about the right way to live, but my version has become more austere than those of most of them.

To judge by the sorts of things that are taught in the national parks or wilderness areas these days, the peripatetic style of a Sharsmith walks seems antique. Interpreters no longer lead day-long hikes in national parks. But my writing and my walking follow in his tradition. In this time when everything seems to be known—but only seems—I attempt to find a better ecology of writing about this activity that no longer pretends to be natural. I attempt to create an aesthetic of this experience and critique it too, along with the inherited modes of representing these mountains.

Taking a walk is no simple thing, and reporting what befalls more difficult than I supposed some time ago. It is too easy to scorn the grim-faced backpackers trudging down the dusty trail to Glen Aulen with their new gear giving them blisters and sores, and too easy to laugh at certain older people wandering in the woods and meadows with their binoculars, bird and flower books, and garden bonnets. But what are we all doing here in this place? What do we expect to learn and what do we expect to be?

What, to put it bluntly, are the grounds for devoting so much time and placing such importance on this matter of traversing rock? And are these valid, useful, tenable grounds? I assert that the ground for my walking is granite, and as indicated earlier, granite is no simple substance. Being on granite puts one in contact with processes at the bottom of what we call the earth.

This sort of talk may seem either mystical or overly academic and yet is remarkably peripatetic—perhaps a digression, but from what? The etymology of this word, digression, leads to *grade, grading,* and *school.* (Consider *courses* and *trails* too, but that is in another chapter.) Though surely not in school when I walk away, as I have done every spring for my entire life, it would be presumptuous to believe I have escaped it. Many teachers always shadow me in the mountains; some may be hidden, like Loren Eiseley's "Hidden Teacher."[6]

Walks are not single in nature, but multivalent: A good one branches and potentially becomes at least as complex as the geographical pattern it enters and the interior map that enters it. The complexity of Tuolumne's geography as perceived by those who travel within it may approach the infinite.

An agenda begins with the questions asked, and these questions are legion. One afternoon I heard Kimi Hill quote her grandfather, Chiura Obata, surely the premier painter of this region. He said, "I like to walk because it exercises my eyes." The questions an artist like Obata asks may not be ours. A musician might say that she likes to walk because it exercises her ears. Writers almost universally and incurably perambulate. The questions we ask direct us to the shapes of our expression.

But walking is also a craft in itself, a mode by which one can disabuse one's self of certain illusions, like the notion of freedom. This is particularly true of mountain walking. On many excursions, I learned how to set a pace, adjust breathing and stepping. We practiced the rest step—or guide's step as it is sometimes called—that synchronizes breath with stride in an almost meditative way. Somewhat later, I met people who dogtrotted along trails, but they did not interest me much. And so I continue to believe that walking is stepping, breathing, and resting. To pace is to stretch out one's legs and to stretch out one's mind, but also to embrace reality, to measure one's world and self.

Eventually, I also led hikes, teaching the same techniques. For many summers when I was a rock climber here, no doubt the discipline of climbing influenced my views of walking.

Because the mountains are not all unbroken rock, I also learned a technique called talus hopping, which is rather more like talus running. For a couple summers I ran trails in this region. I ran trails and climbed rock and now I walk rock and avoid trails. Valerie and I have also skied when snow covered these granite slopes and what we discovered about skiing no doubt influenced our views. As it turned out, there are places where crusted snow will support Valerie but not me.

The nuanced language we use for walking is itself interesting because it reveals subtle differences between ways or modes of human being. We might amble, saunter, stroll, hike, go on a jaunt, stride out, strut, prance, swagger, or even tread the Earth. We might drift or meander, as if we were more like a stream. We might dream or imagine ourselves gliding, floating, or flitting over rock, but once we are moving, we are rarely able to describe our own mode of locomotion exactly with these terms. We might wander or ramble—which is to say, digress.

We might march, traipse, or tramp—and consider the social implications. Traipse was one of my mother's favorite expressions for the reluctant hiking of her young sons. As a child, I also went to peace marches led by Linus Pauling and I aspired to be a chemist. Now, being older, I might pace myself, or stagger in fatigue, slog, reel, sway, wobble, lurch, or pitch. Norman Clyde (1885–1972), the grand old man of Sierra mountaineering, used to speak of taking shank's mare. There are many modes of walking. These change with conditions and can only be imperfectly expressed. Know this: I no longer traipse; I no longer march.

So we are taught to imagine ourselves before, during, and after we set out. In this sense, one might say that, while walking may be the chief daytime activity in Tuolumne Meadows, when we go outside to walk we are still inside inherited dreams and expectations and also inside a tradition and a language that has shaped our own. In more than one sense, I began to go to the Sierra because I wanted to go out of bounds; once I arrived, I found myself within bounds, not just of tradition but of geology—I became a captive though perhaps I desired to be an inhabitant or even a connoisseur of the Tuolumne Intrusive Suite. Yet, as my father used to say, "Just because you want something doesn't necessarily mean you'll get it." The world is a hard place, as hard as granite. One must tread carefully.

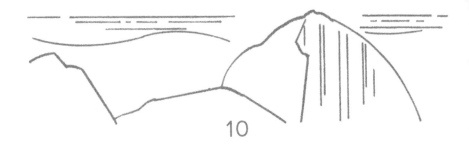

10

Rock and Water

Antiquarian interests. We live in a developed Yosemite.

WE EASILY GET to one of our favorite walks because we wish to look down at Tenaya Creek as it enters its canyon once again. A source of the Merced River, the creek flows out of Cathedral Lakes, through Tenaya Lake, past Clouds Rest, Quarter Domes, Mount Watkins, Half Dome, and Washington Column. Inspecting its flow is often the first thing we do in early spring.

To get to a parking place we must drive the Tioga Road past Olmsted Point—a viewpoint named for him long after his death, along the highway with a large congested parking lot that did not exist when we were children. We drive the road that has been blasted out to deface the flowing granite slabs south of Tenaya Lake. A usual, these glacially polished and shapely slopes are covered with soot from the process of snow removal that occurs every year.[1]

Our parking place itself provides a disappointing scene; it is next to a huge quarry cut into a rocky ridge, seemingly abandoned, and next to that a large lot filled with broken rock, pieces of rusted machinery, and other detritus associated with road construction and maintenance. None of this mess is on any map we have ever seen.

Once we leave the disturbed area, we descend a gentle granite ridge until we can look down upon great water over immense fields of rock, from a great height. Since writing is about memory, memory must be refreshed each year. So be it. Once again we behold a world of Half Dome Granodiorite, more clearly experienced than remembered. There is a newly beaten trail to the top of Mount Watkins, but not to where we are going. We diverge over untracked rock.

We amble past western white pines. Even in late spring, the approach is dry, where we descend gently eroded granite ridges to an overlook. Here rock plunges a thousand feet to Tenaya Creek, and the creek too plunges. Water cascades when it can. What is it to fall like that, I wonder, while Valerie notices a hawk soar below the rim. What we know is a roar of water diminishes to a whisper here on this exposed ledge as it arises and floats in the canyon.

We are on top of a prominence known to climbers as YaSoo Dome, perhaps a name from the Japanese *Yasu*, meaning peaceful or quiet. YaSoo is more a projection of canyon wall than a freestanding rock. Why would anyone be dizzy here, vertiginous, except that great height comes upon us with such suddenness?

From here we can see the cables on Half Dome and, with binoculars, the people ascending and descending them. Sometimes we can even hear the hikers. Indeed, we can see many climbing routes from here, some I have followed. I sometimes say to friends, "I wasted my youth climbing rocks," but know I am lying. I contradict myself often. I think about climbing briefly while I am here. Why not focus on those things that one can approach closely and touch? I yearn to touch them, though every touch is mediated. After all, a climbing route is a representation.

A climbing route might be a narrative that takes a person's body from the bottom to the top of a mountain or cliff. What such a route represents! Ascent itself—to scale, mount, rise, soar, fly. And more: to mark a line upon a mountain that one has etched. At some level one must know that this is foolishness. Climbing routes are cultural narratives, but what is the culture and what narrative is worth telling? A climbing route is a trope, part of a larger so-called vernacular landscape that somehow integrates nature and culture. Like other climbers of my generation, I participated in a few "first ascents," but not many. Mostly, my partners and I repeated other so-called "classic routes," and these experiences were a source of pleasure.[2] None of us pretended that we were in some wilderness. We knew where we laid down our sleeping bags, how we had gotten here, and just how urbanized Yosemite Valley had become.

In any case, Valerie and I also come here to watch spring snow avalanche off Clouds Rest. When we were younger we used to ski by this place in winter on our way from Yosemite Valley to Tuolumne Meadows. Things are scoured now. Snow has done the housekeeping.

Tenaya Creek has always drawn us. From the peaceful flow as it leaves Tenaya Lake and wanders through a forest, it undertakes a first big slide past giant potholes, tumbles down several steeper falls, and cascades below Clouds Rest to drop into a square-cut so-called "inner gorge" and the boulder-filled creek bed below. One might enter this watershed from any of a number of places. All lead across great sheets of granite, each journey satisfactory in itself. Valerie prefers to follow the stream from Tenaya Lake. I like to approach more abruptly, from the steep sides, trucking down the smooth slabs.

According to geologist N. King Huber, "In Tenaya Canyon, Tioga ice was thicker and reached farther up the walls, smoothing them and removing irregularities; no pinnacles and spires are found there."[3] There seem to be few erratic boulders here either. The entire surface of the region is swept clean. Somewhere down in this canyon, John Muir took his only recorded fall on rock. We will not fall from the top of YaSoo Dome but only sit, watch, and listen.

What we see may become a world of drought. Just over the divide, the Tuolumne River too may soon become a world of rock and little water, as the geologist Greg Stock has shown, because the primary source of the river is the Lyell Glacier.[4] When that glacier disappears, as it is likely to do soon, the river will cease to flow through Tuolumne Meadows in late summer or early fall. There will be no source of water after winter snows have melted: The river will go dry as it has never done during my years here. In my time, glaciology in Yosemite approaches an entirely archaeological science.

Tenaya Creek may also cease to flow, as it did in the historically recent past, during the so-called Medieval Warm Period (800–1200 A.D.), when Tenaya Lake turned into what must have been a stagnant pool. Pines grew within the lake basin during this long drought and could again. As one scientist notices, "For the trees to have grown, the lake must have been nearly dry. In contrast, only once during the past 50 years has the lake not overflown during snowmelt."[5]

Now when we think of Tuolumne Meadows, we imagine pure water burbling over smooth granite. This is the rule every spring, we say to ourselves, but we also know that this is a representation just as is the immediacy of coming upon untouched rock here, and touching it. Hand and rock and water; mind and memory and representation. The soft and hard.

Returning ourselves to the present state of affairs, we open our water bottles and drink. When we go walking on rock we must carry our own water these days, for the Sierra's granite will be mostly, and we are guessing increasingly, without water.

Yet rhythms of rock without water always counterpoise with sounds of water running over rock. As a changing climate has become obvious recently, people have begun to notice that some rocks hold water: This has become an essential biological issue. Because granite is not very porous, unbroken it will not absorb water. To put it another way, granite gives up its waters freely.

Yet granite does not offer much in the way of fruitfulness. It is like the cypress Thoreau mentions in the conclusion to "Economy": a tree that does not bear fruit and is thereby free, always flourishing, but "affords nothing to give away." Though granite's pure water is poor in minerals and weak in nutrients, granite streams are not devoid of life but are certainly life-poor. What water offers to us, in spring, is sound.

Though granite may hold water underground in catchment basins below the soil, and broken or weathered granite may increase the retention of water by overlying soil, yet undissected granite is impervious. Glaciers hold water. Glaciers carve lake basins that hold water. But rock without water is the rule where bare granite reigns.

Here on a path of pure unadulterated granite, when there is water, clear water pours over miles of shining rock, sometimes swiftly. Whatever the future holds, this granite will never hold more. Water pours off. Water makes noise. Rock is silent, until it isn't.

So I read a familiar poem again, though what it says is not always true for me here: "Here is Belladonna, the Lady of the Rocks, . . . Which are mountains of rock without water." This one poem expresses an inherited fear of *wasteland*—and it is such an interesting term, a traditional yoking of words whose figurative sense is buried somewhere between the thirteenth and nineteenth century. A waste is empty, desolate, uncultivated, unfit for use—like this very place where we are, some might say. In the meantime, here is water enough, and rock.

The mind always goes somewhere else, where literary figures of a future enumerate, suggesting that comfort may have been a matter of springs or pools among the rocks, that redemption came surely from "the sound of water only," and most certainly the "sound of water over a rock."[6] For the moment, water still cascades, and the sound is enough. Wallace Stegner got one thing right when he referred with reverence to "The Sound of Mountain Water."

We get to our dome by driving the Tioga Road of course, one of the ugliest highways we have ever driven in a national park, through the most beautiful landscape. And only a little while ago I could ride a bicycle to our parking spot. Once a year, on a single day, before the Park Service opens the highway through Tuolumne Meadows to automotive traffic, bicyclists and pedestrians can walk the highway that will be choked by RVs and speeding cars trying to cross the Sierra in a hurry for the rest of the season. On one day every year, one can hear the water and imagine the whole region with only pedestrians, bicyclists, and electric vans. I await that day every year because it reminds me—and Edward Abbey before me—of what a national park could be.

We are not forward thinkers, Valerie and I, and are becoming antiquarians, maybe for the reason our friend Richard White once suggested in a letter, that "as we age we are more and more attracted to things that do not care."

Being particular, maybe eccentric, kinds of antiquarians (who value the old, from the Latin *antiquarius*, "pertaining to antiquity," from *antiquus*, "ancient, aged, venerable"), we look to the ancient not only because it is old, but also because it is venerable, worthy of respect, and a foundation for the present. We increasingly turn our attention to those things humans cannot create—trees thousands of years old, granite mountains beyond human measure, frightening canyons, the continent upon which we live, the Earth, solar system, galaxies, the universe.

To speak of our geological interests as antiquarian is to create a kind of metaphor or analogy to human history, as Martin J.S. Rudwick demonstrates in his masterful book *Bursting the Limits of Time: The Reconstruction of Geohistory in the Age of Revolution*.[7] As he insists, study of geological history has always been analogous to the study of human history—and the latter has shaped the former. Early geologists found the deep past to be a kind of foreign country, calling for erudite and antiquarian inspection and requiring historical explanation.

We have inherited this perspective, asking always, "How did this come to be?" It is hard to know whether our reading supplements physical contact and direct observation of events, processes, and causes—or vice-versa.[8] There is always something more. Experiencing this crucial contact of past with present means coming to grips with what Georges Cuvier, the father of paleontology, called the "revolutions" of the past.[9] We prefer these days to occupy our minds with revolutions of a geological past rather than face revolutions of the political present.

Perhaps our perspective is too narrow and too close-up. Perhaps we should be asking about continents, those "self-restraining" bodies that, by holding together, are continuous, as their etymology suggests: "exercising self-restraint." Only from the 1550s onward was the word *continent* thought of as a large "continuous" landmass, as in the Latin *terra continens*—continents being continent, we hope. Perhaps a longer view in time or space would be comforting.

For instance, there are many old granitic rocks on this Earth, many much older than the rock of Yosemite, and most made of rock older than themselves. Recently, a team of geochemists visited an area near the Hudson Bay, north of Quebec, that they take to be the center of the North American Craton, a geologically stable region where they found rocks they dated by isotopes to be approximately 2.7 billion years old, from the Archean period.

According to Jonathan O'Neil, a geochemist at the University of Ottawa and lead researcher, "A natural recycling process, whereby shifting plates swallowed up pieces of the Earth and spit them back out, created these ancient boulders. This recycling happens about every 250 million years, but the scientists found the original rocks were a lot older than that number would suggest," because "the parent rocks are much, much older, about 1.5 billion years older [or 4.2 billion years old overall]."[10]

Or perhaps we should see Tenaya Canyon from a higher perspective, through more contemporary terms, following certain trends in modern thinking. When the eminent geographer John B. Jackson (1909–1996) redefined or, better still, defined a meaning of landscape for my generation, he reminded us that the word *landscape* originates not with a portion of land that one can view, but with a cultural perspective and particularly an artistic representation of it. And secondly, he turned attention to something that has come to be called "vernacular landscape." Landscape, he wrote, "is *never* simply a natural space, a feature of the natural environment; it is always artificial, always synthetic, always subject to sudden or unpredictable change. We create them and need them because every landscape is the place where we establish our own human organization of space and time."[11] He sometimes visualizes landscape in this way: "It is from the air that the true relationship between the natural and the human landscape is first clearly revealed. The peaks and canyons lose much of their impressiveness when seen from above. What catches our eye and arouses our interest is not the sandy washes and the naked rocks, but the evidences of man."[12]

Not disagreeing with Jackson's important viewpoint, we chose to pursue a perspective that calls for introspection closer to the ground and does not focus on the "evidences of man." Yet surely the itineraries of all walks are structured by representations: a kind of mental infrastructure, unconscious perhaps and learned by heart. The "true relationship between the natural and the human" changes, depending on how we focus. When we go to YaSoo Dome, we have already taken advantage of many of the conveniences, waypoints, and structures that are part of Yosemite National Park, as the granite quarry reminds me.

I admit it: Traditional stonework in Yosemite National Park is often quite beautiful. Even the low retaining walls of rough-hewn granite blocks that border roads leading into Yosemite Valley from the west seem triumphs of masonry. They look as if talus had arranged itself into rectilinear patterns.

Eight attractive granite-faced bridges arch across stream-crossings within the Valley, most built in the 1920s. (Similarly one finds wonderful stone structures in Zion National Park and the Grand Canyon.)

The oldest structures here in the Meadows, many based on native stone, seem the best to us. We have lived or slept in at least four historic buildings, most dating from the 1930s, comfortable within walls buttressed by granite blocks.[13] We have also slept in a log cabin—the oldest inhabited building in the park—and in various campgrounds, though some have moved or closed over the years.

The craftsmanship of these buildings—built of stone and wood—remains impressive and we fondly imagine the Civilian Conservation Corps laborers who were lucky to have employment during those times as they quarried stone. We are not entirely sure where most of the stone was gathered, with the exception of that of the Parsons Lodge, where slabs of granite were quarried on Sierra Club property, right up the hill. These men cut and milled trees, laid them out and put these massively built winter-proof dwellings together. We are told that manual labor was preferred in implementing the CCC projects because it maximized the number of jobs.[14] Now visitors are likely to admire the "hand crafted techniques" of "rustic architecture."[15]

Sometimes, too, we come upon old and abandoned trails that have no clear beginnings or ends, whose granite retaining walls were constructed painstakingly with cut blocks. Yosemite trail building is a craft that calls for understanding the nature of granite. The history of these trails is interesting in itself.[16]

Nevertheless we contend that these walls, structures, trails, and buildings, though necessary, are not the heart of Yosemite, but only provide access, decoration, and accommodation. We have used and appreciate them and hope they will be well preserved. To that extent we might seem to contradict ourselves. Nevertheless, these are not what we have been here for. To make a distinction, though granite may not be sacred, alluvium, talus, moraines, and loose glacial deposits are not the same as rock quarries and gravel pits.

Now, though we pay less attention to Jackson's larger surrounding vernacular landscape when focused on granite, yet we know where the road is, and where the parking lots are, where trails and climbing routes go. Helicopters and airplanes fly overhead. Haze to the west is a result of agriculture and urban pollution. We contend that these are distractions, not a point of convergence. We contend that our way of paying attention clears the mind and makes a home, though global changes lurk somewhere nearby. It is enough to live most of the time in a hazy and noisy traditional vernacular landscape, our house in a city, with elaborate infrastructure and cultural history—where we write letters to our congressmen. For us, home, focus, convergence is found somewhere else.

Anne Whiston Spirn, a scholar I often admire, asks whether everyone's experience of Yosemite is created by human design.

As a case in point, she uses the view from Glacier Point. As she puts it, "Ironically, Olmsted's concealment of the artifice of his intervention (a tradition continued today in the national parks) permits the misconception that places like Yosemite are not designed and managed."[17] Of course they are. It is true that most tourists would not take in the view from Glacier Point or Olmsted Point without driving the road or hiking the Four Mile Trail that takes them to this prospect, but what they see, while gazing across Yosemite Valley from these viewpoints to the north from Glacier Point, or to the south from Olmsted Point, is not created by those roads or trails. And if they wish to go a bit further, they may find things not imagined by framers of national parks.

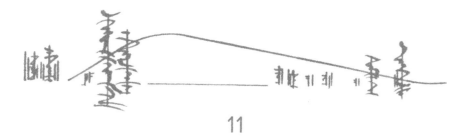

Inside Rock

Why we go outside to visit rock.

This universe henceforth without a master
seems to him neither sterile nor futile.
Each atom of that stone, each mineral flake
of that night-filled mountain, in itself forms a world.
The struggle itself toward the heights
is enough to fill a man's heart.
One must imagine Sisyphus happy."

ALBERT CAMUS, *The Myth of Sisyphus*[1] (emphasis mine)

WE WILL HAVE NO granite countertops in our house. What they have to say offends us, in their rectilinear absurdity, their often ugly and artificial colors, and their human-made shine. We like to eat upon stone, but not inside our own house. When I see these stoned counters in other people's houses, they seem, in their shape and their function, like places of business or places of death. They make me wonder what really counts indoors and outdoors.

Most granite quarried for indoor use comes from India or Brazil, as I have read. Quarried, cut, sliced, laid flat, augmented with resin, sanded and buffed, sold to consumers. Stone broken from rock, brought indoors. Turning rock into stone involves an elaborate fragmentation, including mining, manufacture, transport, and installation. The process seems an abuse or breaking of some higher law for frivolous reasons. The production of stone has always been dangerous to the health of quarriers. The rules of rock are longstanding and healthy by comparison.

Perhaps we are extremists when we say, "Rock belongs outside, burnished by wind and rain and snow." Like others, we go to the Sierra Nevada to study granite in its natural environment. We also go to the Sierra just to be with the granite. It is not the only batholith in the world, but it is our local batholith. Deep rock, risen into the sky, is uplifting. Strangely enough, granite makes us playful and light-minded. This is what our opportunities or privilege have allowed. We walk, climb, study, play, and ski when there is snow.

As the purveyors of kitchen surfaces boast, granite is everywhere and never the same. There is no universal object called granite, but only myriad granitic forms. Though never the same, these granites are similar across countless variations, resembling each other almost as if they pattern an imperfect platonic and plutonic representation of some eternal and timeless idea. One must look for minute differences. One must find a way to avoid the sameness of boredom. One must crystallize, freeze thought, and feel the crust. No granite will tell everything about itself. *"Le secret d'ennuyer est celui de tout dire"* (The secret of being a bore is to tell everything).[2]

Only humans could study granite for what it represents. Who would care to study surfaces where nothing grows? Only us, and not all of us. For some creatures, these slabs are the shortest distance to wherever they are going; we wish them well. Coyotes and recently cougars cross these slabs. (The very word *slab* has an unknown etymology.) I know who has been here from the trail of pointed scat and my dog's focused attention, his sense of smell. He's a little uncomfortable. Smooth granite is not accommodating to claws.

We choose the granites here in Tuolumne Meadows because these are the granites we know. We cannot know all
granites—and even these only imperfectly. What is granite
that so many well-educated people should cultivate it with
such single-minded devotion? We engage in an absurd activity,
rubbing our hands on these surfaces, interesting ourselves in
the inanimate, while deciding to live.

Are we counter-cultural? Or are we consumers, as one of
my friends has argued?[3] I do not think either label applies—yet
both do. Nevertheless, I think our project *is* "work for a living."
Knowing granite is hard work and takes discipline, devotion,
long study. We are not engaged in Joseph Campbell's project
to "follow your bliss," as if "you put yourself on a kind of track
that has been there all the while, waiting for you, and the life
that you ought to be living is the one you are living."[4]

The narrator of *The Dharma Bums* (1958) once said of
Japhy Rider, a devotee of mountains based on Gary Snyder,
"All Japhy's doing is amusing himself in the void."[5] Maybe so.
But neither Snyder nor we are just amusing ourselves and the
mountains are no void to us. We are here to focus. Our work
has always been out of doors.

Our quest is unashamedly mythical. We all live by myths.
What is a myth but speech or thought as story, logical or illog-
ical, delivered by word of mouth or on paper? Camus's myth
is built with the following French diction: *la montagne, les
rochers, cette pierre, pleine de nuit*, and *minéral de cette montagne*. Mountain, rock, stone, and mineral atoms of night: that
form a world. His text influences and shapes itineraries of my
walks. In Camus's myth, "Each atom of that stone, each mineral flake of that night-filled mountain, in itself forms a world."

For instance, on the south ridge of Tuolumne's Johnson
Peak, granite seems to perfect itself as if it were porcelain and
is sometimes called *leucogranite*—something so white and

smooth that it must have been created by life or the petrifi-
cation of snow. In such a light, considering a short scramble
up the ridge above seems pure delight. Nothing this high in
the sky should be so smooth and unblemished. One sneaks
around or reclines amid unspeakable surfaces below relentless
sunlight. It is also called Johnson Granite Porphyry.[6] I call it
lovely and remarkable.

I have chosen to treat rock, and in particular granite, as
if it were something of value that came before us, though it
did not wait for us—as if it were meant to be visited outdoors.
Processes that create rock can only be called "natural," since
they go on without the help of any human hand. Yet they
also seem beyond any distinction between nature and culture: Being beyond human biological timescales, they seem
almost metaphysical. In Yosemite, the scale of these processes
is impressive.

In this mood, I look at the Sierra now and imagine I can
see some soul—but really it is all rock, obdurate naked rock. In
some strange sense these grainy heights have become an ideal,
both of rock with water and rock with no water. The High
Sierra seems now like a trace of the past left after a different
era has retreated, and so it is. In the last few years a drought-
ridden Sierra became "anthroposcenic," as Bill Fox, a friend of
mine, says. As in a Wallace Stevens world where grass rattles,
trees drop their needles: "Here in the midst of the bad," one
reads in a Stevens poem.[7]

Sierra Nevada! Where did the Nevada go? Not into the im-
maculate heart of rock. There is a lot of rubble in the Sierra,
as Valerie points out. In the view from atop Mount Barcroft
high in the White Mountains, the Sierra looks, on its surface,
to be about one-eighth naked rock, capping a huge mound of
eroded dirt foothills and moraines, either barren or covered
with brush and forest.

In the midst of the Sierra's apotheosis of rock, snow becomes only a memory. Sometimes I travel rock-filmed with dust and ashes and accommodate myself to drought, saying foliage was always only decorative. Smoke everywhere. Nevertheless, I remember very clearly the way I would relax, back when I spent my time climbing high peaks—and in particular in an area called Granite Park, above Bishop California's Pine Creek—when each afternoon I would descend to little meadow-fringed lakes and forests, sensing the relief of being with growing things. What plants remain here in the Sierra Nevada are satisfactory, better than us. Something in a plant knows the ephemeral, throwing off seeds and spores as if there will be a tomorrow.

As anyone can tell from these foregoing flights of rock, I read Emerson too early and too uncritically. But when hard pressed I will say this: I trust rock because doing so does not require me to imagine that it is anything but rock, Snyder's line often with me. "No one loves rock, yet we are here." I think my friend Jon Christensen put this case well when he told me that he did not love the Great Basin of Nevada, but he found it interesting. I find rock interesting; I find its forms arresting. I spend as much time as I can exercising that interest—playing with the forms rock has taken—according to my physical and mental capabilities. When I read the many moralistic arguments for and against so-called wilderness and what we used to think of as the natural, I turn away to this rock that has no consciousness, being before and beyond culture or morality. These rocks, that I might secretly say I love, continue to exfoliate, and I do not expect to find their center or essence.

I admit it: We wilderness advocates were wrong, believing as we did that the wild is what we cannot alter—but we were not wrong when we insisted that we should dare not. Now that we no longer imagine we can preserve anything, we also know that none of our gardens will last a season. What remains will be like these unforgiving rocks, like tombstones, surfaces about which we have so little knowledge. This rock, too hot or too cold to touch, how can it be managed or utilized? Consider the galaxies, whose rocks we will never touch.

The evolution of rock has not been like the evolution of life. Yet rock is everywhere, ubiquitous and eternal. These cliffs and pavements will outlast us. Their surfaces seem permanent, though they are not. And yet they renew themselves.

Rock cannot speak; it has no language. Rock cannot represent itself, though plants and animals can and do represent themselves, to themselves and to others. We call rock obdurate because of our ideas of hardness and persistence. We call it obdurate because it is mute. Like a picture with no depth, it suggests nothing but its surface. Yet sculpture, too, as art historians have pointed out, is absolutely nothing but surface. Because we are humans, every surface always suggests depth. A surface always invites the observer to insert himself into its depths. One secret of meditative calmness is to hide this suggestion from yourself—and in my case go out the granite backdoor, as it were.

When I was climbing, we used to have twin expressions: face climbing and crack climbing. I was good at the first and practiced it for many years, learning to ascend on the smallest of edges, practicing delicacy, as if the rock were skin. But I discovered I was better at the second and more strenuous technique, especially ascending the interior of what we called squeeze chimneys, where one inserted one's body into steep fissures.

These are and are not sexual metaphors. However, one hears about books that claim that "The Stones Begin to Speak," only to discover that the text is about what humans have written upon surfaces. I myself have written upon the rocks, but I always preferred to do so with invisible ink because I am not the first climber of Tuolumne granite, nor do I hope to be the last. Yet climbing is inescapably a kind of writing.

The notion of granite as monumental stone—as marker, memorial, tombstone, headstone, gravestone—though obsessive and faintly repellant, dogs me. The rock Sisyphus pushes remains in motion. So, in a larger sense, do these. I let the domes of Yosemite, the plutons that formed this region, be my markers.

Though I am no longer a climber, I continue to abide with rock whenever I can and for as long as I can. Sometimes I wander below the faces of cliffs. I suppose one might say that I wait, fall behind, and dwell in some plutonic past. The rock has cooled millions of years ago, of course, but I have not yet.

In this context, what does it mean to trust rock, or trust yourself? What does it mean to trust anything? That something is safe, strong, reliable. This obdurate element, this rock, draws out obdurateness. Like rock, I say, though I test each handhold or foothold. I do not trust myself entirely, but desire to do so.

As my body grows older, its parts seem sometimes to petrify. My face has weathered, my skin roughened and pitted, speckled with imperfections; my joints creak. This erosion that comes from within and is hastened by forces beyond my control is both like and unlike the erosion of rock.

Though pieces fall off, the body of granitic rock does not rot, does not bend to the wind, does not reproduce, does not care about change. Rock endures. Rock does not change its expression. Rock has no expression except the names and faces we give it and the stories we tell about it.

Right and Wrong Kinds of Rock

Granite versus other rocks.

Books are for the scholar's idle times.
When he can read God directly
the hour is too precious to be wasted
in other men's transcripts of their readings.

RALPH WALDO EMERSON, "On the American Scholar"

WE BELONG TO A group Jon Krakauer names "aficionados of the continental crust," mountain walkers and climbers who prefer "granite and its closest igneous cousins" and dismiss everything else as "country rock."[1] These granites, we say, are the right rocks. Valerie ceased walking on the metamorphic slopes of Mount Dana long ago.

Krakauer's right rocks, according to the *Encyclopedia Britannica*, are "deep-seated plutonic rocks" denuded or pushed up by tectonic forces, or both. Nevertheless, "intrusive rocks have cross-cutting contacts with the country rocks that they have invaded." So the best rock comes from depth, is most coherent, is the stuff of greatness, the nude intruder. Over, under, and sometimes cutting through granitic intrusions, we encounter country rocks that "show evidence of having been baked and thermally metamorphosed at these contacts."

As a necessary economic diversion—lasting about thirty years—we spent nearly half of our lives in exile from granite in Southern Utah, and we became interested in the many-layered tale of sediments that comprises the Colorado Plateau. The sedimentary rock of the Colorado Plateau is like a book, leaf upon leaf, chapter after chapter. The sandstone in the Colorado Plateau is wonderful for walking or climbing, but also because it is part of a legible historical sequence. You can walk right into this book. Everything that happens to Yosemite granite reveals itself more precisely on its surface. Sandstone does not preserve its surfaces so well, but it does preserve its form.

A favorite layer for us and for many other walkers and climbers is the Navajo Sandstone. Navajo Sandstone exfoliates to forms similar to granitic ones, and in particular, exfoliation creates monumental arches in places like Zion National Park. What is Navajo Sandstone that its grains hold the memory of their silica origins?

Navajo Sandstone is the most massive bed of rock on the Colorado Plateau. It has a more readable history than granite because it is not igneous. But of course, like all sandstone, Navajo Sandstone reveals various kinds of evidence that it has been recycled, while granite attempts to hide its origins. Granite is young rock: Cretaceous, maybe only one hundred million years old.

Sandstone is quite different underfoot, and that matters a great deal for walkers. We are fond of sandstone. It is a right kind of rock for walking, grainy like sandpaper, so the feel and gait are different. During many forays during our sandstone era and ever after, Valerie and I have been arguing about the virtues of massive Navajo Sandstone versus massive granite. This argument has gone on for so long a time that we believe it will never end. We have reached no conclusion. As our friend David Craig once wrote in *Native Stones*, "Rock is everywhere we are not, the hardest thing to be. We have to approach it knowing it is unyielding and that our fantasies steam back off it."[2]

Somehow Navajo Sandstone and its other sedimentary cousins do not fit into the Krakauer dichotomy. Probably twice as old as Yosemite granite, its formation is dated to the Late Triassic or Early Jurassic from sand deposited about 190 million years ago. It originated when there was only one continent and one ocean on Earth.

Granite is not like sandstone—it was not laid down but welled up. Granite does not suggest any repose or any chronological narrative of "formations," as do the layers of the Colorado Plateau, but instead burst up, insisting on great power. Granite is the stuff of the right kind of mountains because one imagines, rightly or wrongly, that it rises inexorably from the depths.

Perhaps there is such a thing as the wrong kind of rock. Once I went on a walk—never mind where—and ended up in a place with the wrong kind of rock. The creeks were shrouded in vegetation. The footing was unstable. I hated it there. Any rock can show a welcoming or an intimidating face. Or consider the lava of Mauna Loa, the *pahoehoe* and *a'a*. The first appears smooth but is as rough as a kitchen grater. One cannot slide on this rock. *A'a* is so rough and jagged that one avoids it altogether. Lately we have been treading limestone and dolomite while in search of old or impressive subalpine trees in the Great Basin—the right kind of rock for those trees but the wrong kind for our ankles.

Almost universally, mountain climbers speak of their "home range," where they travel comfortably and confidently, and for many where they learned their craft. For us that is the Sierra Nevada of California. Consequently, the granite of the Sierra is fundamental for us, I say, classifying myself as a classifier. The foundation, the primary principle, the lowest note of a rich chord. Elemental, this ground. Consequently, we always considered the sedimentary world a kind of exile and returned to granite late each spring as the snow melted, only retreating to the monumental sandstone each fall.

Indeed, for some time geologists believed that granite was *the* "fundamental rock mass," primary, because it seemed to underlie all others.[3] This is so intuitive and antiquarian—to believe in granite's primacy, to trust its solidity, to imagine it as the home range for all of us. Granite seems eternal, gives a sense of well-being, not like that fragile, friable country rock or volcanic rock that looks like it arrived yesterday (and so it did), a hot light-sink, very sharp, uninteresting, fragmented. Nobody would want to touch magma with a naked hand.

No wonder people prefer sculpted granite domes, pinnacles, cirques, glacial streams. We like our granite highly refined; we walk beside granite-banked streams because they are so clear and unblemished; we dwell, tarry, linger here in the granite headwaters of the Tuolumne River. As the very complicated history of this word *dwell* suggests, it is hard to know whether ours is a story of deception, error, or home-making. For many reasons, granite is a literary rock, a wordy substance filled with complications and ambiguities, difficult to articulate or divide into distinct parts for clarity.

Because people make a place in the world by making a story of a place, stories of granite inhabit that no-man's-land between poetry and science. We live by myths, but every story is not a simulacrum. Does the rock of Sisyphus never break? Why not?

Sometimes one can even choose to participate in someone else's stories and myths. Because Gary Snyder named a place in his poem "Piute Creek"—where he wrote, "No one loves rock, yet we are here"—we could go to the site of his long-eradicated trail camp and follow his footsteps many years later. As if it were yesterday, we traveled downstream, following the watercourse from Benson Lake to Snyder's old stomping ground, the rhythm of granite in this tributary stream, sculpted and pocketed, rough and smooth underfoot.[4]

As a reader, I have always contemplated other people's granite. As congressman William Kent of California wrote of Muir, "With him, it is me and God and the rock where God put it, and that is the end of the story."[5] Like Muir and not like Muir, we have positioned ourselves with respect to the immutable positions of rock, but not so much with respect to god.

One would prefer that rock offer something simpler and less complicated than live beings do. Nobody talks about communities of rocks. Hence igneous interrelationships are referred to with the term "suite," a related set or a sequence of musical pieces. Sandstone is spoken of as in a succession or series. Their relationships of proximity reveal relationships in time. Also nobody eats rocks on purpose, though we will all eat our peck of dirt before we die, as Valerie's grandfather used to say.

Why do I seek out these complications of granite? Because they do not speak and will not argue: The world is solid and it absorbs stories about itself, though as my friend says, may wear them lightly. Anyone might choose the silence and serenity of glacially shaped domes; they might find solace in strong silence. There may be an end to life as humans know it, but not to minerals. Yet see how the words pile up like talus at the bottom of a slope.

All of this is why I prefer rock in place, not moved, cut, made into something else: I prefer to confront bare facts, impartial, unforgiving. I spend a lot of time thinking about these rocks, glaciers, weather, what happens every day on the surface of the earth; I am interested in snowstorms, avalanches, the way things fall, the way things happen, and the changes in these happenings. Though their stories are always with me, people don't matter as much as they used to. To paraphrase and distort William Stafford's line, what the rock says, I say. What the rocks mean is a different matter.

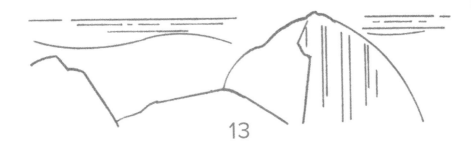

An Aristotelian Mythology of Geohistory

Myth meets science in granite.

WHAT ROCKS MEAN is a geological question, answered through narrative. As I speak of walking on these mountains—and normally I spend more time thinking than speaking—I imagine this narrative in Aristotelian terms. Consider his categories: plot (*mythos*), character (*ethos*), thought (*dianoia*), diction (*lexis*), and to a lesser extent melody (*melos*) or spectacle (*opsis*). After all, Aristotle is the original peripatetic philosopher: He walked while he lectured.

Myth and science establish different ways of understanding "plot," of constructing a story. Explicating mythos requires not just establishing sequence but also exploring the way a narrative creates structure and causality. Consequently, to proceed through any historical construction of geological events ineluctably requires some sense of the history of geological science. Even geologists suffer over distinctions between myth and science. According to William R. Dickinson (1931–2015), a formidable figure who studied plate tectonics and sedimentary geology and was an expert on the geology of the Colorado Plateau:

> Distinguishing between myth and science is subtle, for both seek to understand the things around us. The characteristic style of mythic thinking is to place special

emphasis on a selective conjecture, based typically on the initial observation or recognition of a phenomenon, which is thereafter given privileged status over alternate interpretations. . . . Geomyths stimulate investigation, but also may retard further progress by dismissing contrary views. Improved understanding of geologic history could be attained more efficaciously by appreciating the mythic quality of many nascent ideas in geoscience, and resisting the temptation to accord geomyths favored status over competing hypotheses.[1]

A premier expert on the formation of the Pacific Cordillera, part of the mountains that line the western coast of our continent, Dickson also demonstrated that the sand of Navajo Sandstone originated in the Appalachian Mountains. His quandary about myth and science could be anyone's, but never so well expressed.

We all hold personal geomyths, which bond us to place. For instance, I believe that granite mountains chose me, that this happened early and completely in Tuolumne Meadows. Consequently, I followed many pilgrimages, spread myself around in the world of granite, in the Alaska Range, Wind Rivers, Tahquitz Rock, the Gorge of Despair, the San Juan Rockies, the Hindu Kush of Afghanistan. But also, wandering in these granite mountains entailed a kind of tension between work and play that has become a law, almost peripatetic. My literary exertions and Valerie's artistic expressions have required some knowledge of the structure and history of this and other sierras. Our play has been to live among mountains, climb rocks, evaporate our selves on the heights, and revel in what I might call sculptural flow. Consciously or not, we have immersed our own history in the geomythology and geohistory of these regions.

"Geohistory" in turn, as Martin J. S. Rudwick explains, is "the immensely long and complex history of the Earth." It is no coincidence that his most comprehensive narrative of geological science commences in 1786 with the story of an ascent of Mont Blanc—glacier-enshrouded, made of granite, the highest peak in the Alps. Why would anyone choose to make such an ascent "without even being certain that men could live in the places they aspired to reach"?[2]

A history of human investigations into geohistory might begin with this ascent, where climbing summits is a means, not an end. The purpose of such exploits is imagined to be associated with the construction of knowledge, as Rudwick puts it, synchronously with construction of maps—depictions of relationships and connections that are not simply acquired by comprehensive views from the summit, but that inform human structuring, patterning, designing. These geologists not only depicted on paper the regions of granite and ice visible from the summits, but also made "maps" that connected and related regions of knowledge or disciplines—maps that show how to get from one inquiry to another, following the shape of their relations.

Climbing was, at one time, an all-encompassing discipline for me, yet in a certain sense I chose this occupation to flee from geoscience, to choose a better weekend alternative than geology field trips. I followed an alternate geomythic dream, climbing rocks for much of my youth. Life is not synchronic but inescapably diachronic: One moves on or is moved on— toward wisdom, perhaps.

Maybe I said that badly. Climbing was a discipline—as in instruction, correction, training, order. Climbing was the most demanding mental and physical activity of my youth. Now that I no longer attempt difficult climbs, in this sense I have lost the discipline. Yet granite is not a memory, nor is it only a narrative: It is not one character but many. It tests my diction and thought, becoming an ever-present focus for my attention. If it is not bedrock, it still feels like bedrock to me. I prowl the prows of small domes at dawn as if I were on the deck of a ship, floating on some pluton that continues to rise into the sky, looking into a possible future, asking what discipline(s) might replace the climbs of my past.

A geological perspective probably undercuts the importance of my climbing or of anyone's climbing. The brief history of mountaineering in the Sierra Nevada represents really only a tiny moment in this range's history, hardly an original or best use, as I thought when I was young.[3] In my lifetime, the sport of climbing has fostered many businesses, even an industry, and that does not cheer me either. When I worked for a climbing guide service in Yosemite named the Yosemite Mountaineering School, we sold a T-shirt that said "Go Climb a Rock." I began to realize that my climbing and the stories of my generation will have only a brief, ephemeral significance, mostly to a few friends and myself.

Unlike Allen Ginsberg or William Carlos Williams, neither I nor the geologists desire "through metaphor to reconcile / the people and the stones."[4] The earth is already sufficiently composed and geology desires to know its story. My lesser desire is to explore modes of being in this realm. Nothing needs inventing, I say, and no rocks need splitting. Valerie and I claim to care about the wholeness of granite regions because of the many ways they allow any person to wander silently among their glistening shapes. In this sense we wax mythic.

There seems nothing tumultuous about these stony places. There is nothing disturbed or excited here. It is as if the world were in repose, which is of course not true. These rocks are pure and smooth, impermeable, finished, permanent. Glacial pavements, their surfaces devoid of soil. An occasional glacial erratic, stranded when the ice melted out from under it. Glacial. Like me—I sometimes wish.

Polished igneous rock—that permanent, burnished, monolithic, eternal local granite—provides perspective, masters the walker in me. Rock is what I seek to have a sense of self—not trees or flowers, fish or mammals, not the sounds of birds— only pure clean rock, even if some think of it as the stuff of tombstones, not to be trifled with. I choose rock because it is obdurate and has no life, no change, no feelings; I choose to climb upon it because the act requires a certain kind of self-consciousness, not too much reflection but neither simply doing in the moment. My generation discovered that there must be an ethics associated with the treatment of rock and mountains, so that others may experience them in undamaged form. We called it "clean climbing."[5]

To speak of granite in this way is to speak, if not of the heart, then from something close to the heart of the Sierra— and to speak of what remains of my heart too. I am massively wrong about questions of change because there is always a history of everything, and self-consciousness follows as a consequence. Aristotle called this moment of knowing again or examination *anagnorisis*—"recognition." He was trying to explain the structure of Tragedy.

The Purity of Granite

Is there such a thing as pure granite?

"Scientists still aren't sure how we might have gotten from an early solid crust to our present-day tectonic plates. 'That's the $64,000 question,' says Michael Brown, a geologist at the University of Maryland . . ."[1] Because for some the personal is the geological, I return to geoscience. The preceding epigraph attempts to digest a short but pungent argument found in the journal *Nature*, namely that "Earth's first stable continents did not form by subduction."[2] According to Brown, "during the Archean Eon—spanning 4 billion years ago to 2.5 billion years ago—the Earth's upper mantle was much hotter than it is today, and our planet was highly volcanic." As the coauthored paper argues:

> This protracted, multistage process for the production and stabilization of the first continents—coupled with the high geothermal gradients—is incompatible with modern-style plate tectonics, and favours instead the formation of TTGs [tonalite–trondhjemite–granodiorite rocks] near the base of thick, plateau-like basaltic crust. Thus subduction was not required to produce TTGs in the early Archaean eon.

Out of this different world, I want to ask, "How, when, and why did plate tectonics begin?" And one answer would seem to be, "It is unlikely that plate tectonics began on Earth as a single global 'event' at a distinct time, but rather it is probable that it began locally and progressively became more widespread from the early to the late Archean."[3] Sometime around 2.5 to 4 billion years ago, the earth had cooled enough for continents to form and so began the process of differentiating minerals on the earth's crust that are presently available for study.

When trying to picture an Earth that did not behave as it has in the last few billion years, imagination is stretched. This world lacked free oxygen and water. One thing is sure: Any granite in that world was not produced by the same means as more recent plutons. By this reckoning of time and process, our granite is a relatively new inhabitant of Earth, born in an emerging physico-chemical environment. And there is every reason to believe that granite, in this sense, is neither original nor pure. It must be a result of what Brown calls "crustal reworking." To put this case succinctly: On the one hand, "continental crust is the archive of Earth history," yet on the other hand, "plate tectonics resulted in a biased preservational record."[4]

Granite is neither pure, nor original, nor eternally present, and what can be observed now is itself a complicated and perhaps biased record or archive. To put this in the context of a mountaineer's experience, just as there is no such thing as pure friction climbing, indeed there is no such thing as a pure experience of granite either. How much granite is derived from recycled crustal rocks is by no means clear, but certainly some substantial percentage.[5]

During the evolution of the lithosphere, everything changes: Petrology—the study of igneous, sedimentary, metamorphic rocks and their formation—becomes fluid. In this reality, granite is ultra-metamorphic. Below the crust, under the pressure of change, everything that rises to the surface of the earth has undergone shape-shifting and alteration: Everything is old and new. As Brown puts it, "Thus, metamorphic petrology is concerned with decoding the mineralogical and microstructural record of burial/heating and exhumation/cooling imprinted on preexisting sedimentary, igneous and metamorphic rocks by processes such as subduction, accretion, trench advance or retreat, collisional orogenesis and orogenic collapse."[6] Call these rocks avatars: concrete embodiments of something abstract, something that has ascended from within Earth. Call granite an avatar of a new world, a concrete manifestation of an abstract concept.[7]

Just as, in more prosaic terms, one might say that granite is not so much new as recycled, so too each human, as a cultural and biological being, is recycled from previous constituents of the Earth, in multiple and complex ways. To stretch this simile, I note that people have been treading on granite for quite a long time so that many of my experiences are recycled from innumerable traditions of mountain walking and mountain climbing. (That I began as a hiker, engaged for some time in more serious mountain climbing, and now have returned to mountain walking, might illustrate an answer to the riddle of the Sphinx: "What walks on four legs in the morning, two legs at noon and three at close of day?")

Rock can be brittle, yet nevertheless holds together better than anything else in this life. I have had to realize finally that there is absolutely no possibility of permanence, or purity, or an "original relation to the universe." Which universe? Which eon? Which time of day?[7]

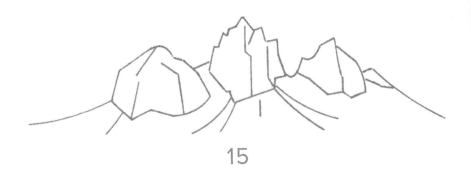

A Contingent Earth

Geologists' stories change, but Earth does not repeat itself.

WHAT MIGHT BE the most gleeful review of Rudwick's monumental historical volumes makes this distinction: "By history of the Earth or geohistory, Rudwick does not mean an awareness of time or of a long timescale: he means the use of surviving relics to infer that in the past there had been a sequence of contingent, unique, and unrepeated events and distinctive periods, both of which were undeducible and unpredictable from general principles."[1]

High up in the watershed the Tuolumne River, in Yosemite National Park, I awaken to one meaning for geohistorical contingency, perceiving these forms, this rock in this place, as part of a unique, incomplete, and potentially unknowable sequence of unanticipated and unrepeatable events, never to come again. Though glaciers shaped this region and may come again, their effects will be different. What is it like to think glacially, to be worn down, plucked from the perspective that everything is exactly in some preordained and perfectly assembled landscape?

Rudwick's two-volume history ends with the discovery of the glacial age of the Pleistocene. Throughout, he argues that within a few decades in the early nineteenth century, "geology became the first truly *historical* natural science; and that it did so as a result of deliberately transposing methods and concepts from the human sciences of history itself."² Geohistory is rooted in conceptions of human history—and vice versa. As my friend says, history entered nature through geology.

It is an embarrassment to think of one's self as partially a nineteenth-century person. Also, though I am not now a geologist, I once trained to be one before turning away. Still, my own mythos must be informed by the geohistorical, as defined by the eminent Japanese geochemist Minoru Ozima. "Earth science is . . . characterized by the fact that certain terrestrial phenomena occur only once in time," he argues; and, as I repeat his words, "occur only on this Earth and only once in time."³ This is a human lesson of some importance to anyone. As to mixing geological history and human history, how can one not?

The "savants," as Rudwick's geologists called themselves, reconstructed the history of nature, "bursting the limits of time," as he writes, "to recover an unexpected sequence of 'worlds before Adam'—by integrating their exploration of mountains and volcanoes, rocks and fossils, with their own understanding of their own lives, lived in social worlds that likewise had been their own *histories*."⁴

This would seem to be a universal phenomenon. Like Rudwick's geologists, my contemporary geochemists and geophysicists were forced to change their opinions. By seeing crucial specimens and localities for myself, even I have been engaged in what geologists call fieldwork. As Rudwick puts it: "Fieldwork was not just a symbolic activity establishing a geologist's stamina and virility," but an experience that could "change their minds in the face of what they saw with their own eyes, *in the field*."⁵

Because we live in social worlds, changing one's mind is a prelude to changing the minds of others by offering landscape views, drawings, engravings, lithographs; as *proxy* specimens, these genres are "as deeply rhetorical (in the proper non-pejorative sense), as their accompanying texts." "Controversy," Rudwick argues, "is not an embarrassing blemish on the fair face of Science, as some scientists seem to feel, but what animates it and gives it life." But controversy has too frequently been presented as a set of polar opposites (Vulcanists vs. Neptunists, Uniformitarians vs. Catastrophists, Evolutionists vs. Fixists), and as Rudwick notes "these seductively simple polarities are deeply misleading." Controversy ought to be more like conversation.[6]

This is my part of a conversation. I may not be an authority but truly believe that some "contingent, unique, and unrepeated events" that "occur only on this Earth and only once in time" sometimes result in places of unspeakable importance. Only once geologically but more than once as human experience—or why do so many people pour into Yosemite? We repeat the same walks, to the same places, to the top of the same peaks many times, some yearly. Space out of mind and back into mind, each time. Just as humans might "burst time," so too they might also "burst place." But should they? As for myself, I have modest aims to know this place and its history.

On any given day, Valerie and might I come upon a small group of people standing in Tenaya Canyon, their figures wavering as if in a reflector oven. These are not the ones we saw drinking beer and playing in the water slide, who were drawn to this place by an article in the local paper that told them how to get here and what sliding equipment to buy. These folk are trying to get a reading on the stresses within the granite above Pywiack Falls. They are thinking with the earth and we converse with them in this vast and unspeakably dazzling amphitheater of complex, variegated granitic intrusion. Later I will follow their work at conferences and in journals.[7]

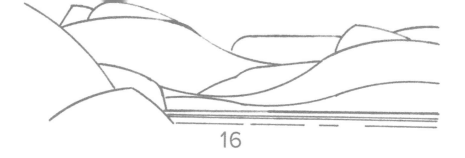

Myths of Glaciers

Imagining a glacial Yosemite.

History is not the past, nor is it events;
it is a shaped conception of the past existing in the present.

EDWARD D. IVES[1]

To be an American (unlike being English or
French or whatever) is precisely to imagine
a destiny rather than to inherit one;
since we have always been,
insofar as we are Americans at all,
inhabitants of myth rather than history.

LESLIE A. FIEDLER[2]

WITH GLACIERS, one begins to think about recent, fresh evidence in geohistory. N. King Huber (1926–2007) was for many years de-facto geologist for Yosemite National Park. He writes, "Hetch Hetchy Valley on the Tuolumne is a much 'fresher' glaciated valley than is Yosemite Valley." Hetch Hetchy was filled to the brim with glacial ice as recently as fifteen to twenty thousand years ago during the so-called Tioga glaciation. According to Huber, Yosemite Valley probably has not been filled for more than 750,000 years, during the Sherwin glaciation. "Thus the upper reaches of

Yosemite Valley cliffs have been shaped by spalling rather than by glacial scour and are much more irregular than those in Hetch Hetchy."[3]

High up in the glaciated watershed of the Tuolumne River in Yosemite National Park, one might be mindful of this history of thinking about glaciation. This rock, in this place, has been shaped by glaciers through "a sequence of contingent, unique, and unrepeated events and distinctive periods," never to come again. What is it like to think this way? Glaciers may not change minds, but as one anthropologist asks, "Do they listen?"[4] They certainly change the regions they inhabit. I care about glaciers because of what they have done in Yosemite. Myths of glaciers indeed.

We choose our stories and our myths. In "Milton by Firelight: Piute Creek, August 1955," Gary Snyder writes:

> In ten thousand years the Sierra
> Will be dry and dead, home of the scorpion.
> Ice-scratched slabs and bent trees.
> No paradise, no fall,
> Only the weathering land . . .[5]

This myth we are now ready for, a myth also enacted in small, season after season. Now there are just shapes of dry water-courses and peaks, sculpted rocks, grooves on granite slabs, and the signs of past water flowing. The glaciers are gone; they did their work, one might say—they unEarthed this place, or so John Muir's mythology goes.

Rock offers something austere, simpler and less complicated than live beings, but narratives of glaciers often make them into animate characters. To imagine glaciers is not the same as to be interested in glaciation. There used to be more glaciers in Yosemite. To that extent, I'm interested in what is happening now—and mostly to me. From the Mammoth Peak, or the west ridge of Mount Gibbs, one looks west toward the coast, senses a movement and power so evident: The flow of past forces, now manifested by a flow of forms, of rock, river, and air.

Because glaciers are part of a narrative and memory someone might seek to recover, in this sense they are mythic. Where I live, you have to travel a good long way to get to one, much of the journey on foot. It used to be that they were not so inaccessible, but I was younger then. Now one thinks about them largely in their absence. In their absence, one looks for signs of their passing.

Valerie and I, in the present, are like ranger naturalists without clients: We are unofficial interpreters of this place. We kneel down on the polished granite and examine the scratches that reveal the direction of flowing ice. We admire the perched erratic boulders. We consider the confirmation of the hills, peaks, and valleys that surround us. We climb small domes and survey the landmarks. We study the shapes of moraines. This is thinking about the glaciers. We picture them in our minds.

Our engagement is not science, but is a matter of finding ourselves in finding out about a place. Our behavior has a history: Just as geology is history, there is also a history of geological thinking and study. Which leads me to say: The glaciers of the Sierra are not here but they will always be here.

Maybe they are in hiding. We offer to welcome them back when they choose to return, as they surely will—though we will not be here to greet them. But we also construct them in our imagination by reading and by studying, using the methods of our teachers.

When Francois Matthes mapped and established a glacial history of Yosemite in 1930, he named the "Ancient Glaciers of the Yosemite Region" as if they were characters in a narrative of becoming (see figure 16.1). The glaciers of what he named the Wisconsin stage include Yosemite Glacier, Merced Glacier, Tenaya Glacier, Snow Creek Glacier, Hoffmann Glacier, glaciers

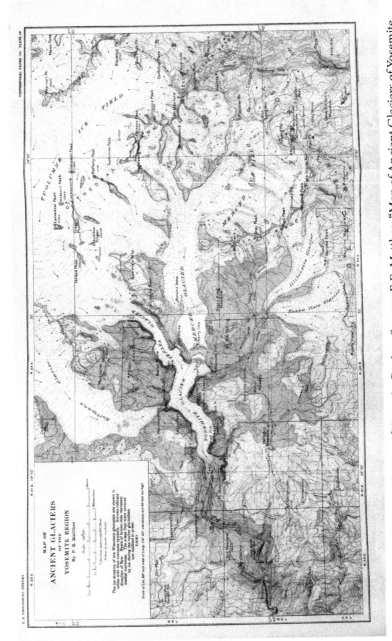

FIGURE 16.1. Map of Ancient Glaciers of Yosemite Region. Source: F.E. Matthes, "Map of Ancient Glaciers of Yosemite Region," US Geological Survey, 1930

of the Illilouette Basin, and glaciers of Bridalveil Basin. He spoke of the upper limit of glaciation in the High Sierra, of the icefields of the past. Later geologists speak of Tahoe and Tioga glaciations, maximums about 130,000 and 20,000 years ago, as equivalent to Matthes's "Wisconsin" glacial stage.

Names of glacial ages of the Sierra Nevada continue to proliferate: Hilgard, Tioga, Tenaya, Tahoe, Mono Basin, Casa Diablo, Sherwin, McGee, Deadman Pass.[6] You see that names of glaciers and names of their ages—or times—may be referenced by names of the places that surround an observer in and about the Sierra, long after the glaciers have melted. Which comes first, place or name, presence or absence?

Muir once reported that "the Indians regard glaciers as living creatures," and maybe he did too.[7] One might also regard them as ghosts. Spatially someone might ask, "where are you?" and I answer from a dream, "on a terminal moraine . . . on a lateral moraine," "above the bergschrund now," and a few minutes before, "below the bergschrund"—or so I used to be able to answer.

Erratics, Domes, and Trundling

Unmoved and moving rocks.

As a huge Stone is sometimes seen to lie
Couched on the bald top of an eminence;
Wonder to all who do the same espy,
By what means it could thither come, and whence . . .

WILLIAM WORDSWORTH, "The Leech Gatherer" (1807)

WE IDENTIFY A BOULDER as an erratic when we think it was transported and deposited by a glacier, partly because it seems to have a mineral structure or origin—a lithology—different from the bedrock upon which it sits. Sometimes in a granitic region these are subtle differences, there being so many kinds of granitic rocks. Erratics sit in unlikely places, above the flow of streams, on top of prominences. But we also often recognize erratics by their surprising and strangely flattened sides because many erratics bear the marks of their journeys, with strangely worn and sometimes polished facets from travelling within glaciers or the waters that poured into their edges. Erratics can therefore reveal patterns of former water or ice flows.

They are also remarkable in themselves. Wandering among the fields of erratics allows for a certain kind of aesthetic experience, informed by knowledge. This experience is not the same in all glaciated places and has changed radically as geological knowledge has evolved. Consequently this aesthetic experience has a unique history.

Some erratics break up and disappear, but rarely those made of granite. Down toward the slopes above Yosemite Valley, some erratics sit on pedestals where the pavement below them has weathered away. People have been fascinated with these long-lived stranded objects, by fields of erratics, for thousands of years. These are literary and perhaps even religious rocks. As one historian puts it, erratic blocks "caught the eye of science" only sometime in the eighteenth century.[1] This is not to say that erratics were invisible before then.

The name for these boulders itself is antique and anachronistic. Erratic, like many good words, comes directly from Latin: *erraticus*, "wandering, straying, roving," and underneath is *erratum*, "an error, mistake, fault." Only more recently do people speak of an erratic as irregular or eccentric. These boulders at first seem mistakenly placed. Used as an adjective—as in "these erratic boulders"—the term suggests that, like landmarks in Homer's *Odyssey*, they are wandering, moving, or even vagrant.

There is a literature about sitting by erratics. According to the Goethe scholar Jason Groves:

> Goethe's writing about these objects is so fascinating because a "glacial age" was only a fuzzy hypothesis, and yet he thought it through and explored some of its consequences in his fictions. The word "erratic" or its German equivalent "erratisch" was not known to him, but he performs this object's erraticness in his inconsistent terminology. He didn't know what to name them; like Mephistopheles in *Faust 2* he can only say "Da liegt der Fels, man muss ihn liegen lassen [As wise men know, it surpasses their reason. / The rock lies evermore where it has lain]."[2]

Groves also recognizes Goethe's sense of the acoustic space of granite "as a tension-filled one: The tension of what cannot be spoken, heard, written, or read, where the muteness (*Stummheit*) of things refers back to the act of a mutation (*Verstummelung*)."[3]

According to the *Oxford English Dictionary*, the term erratic was first used in a geological sense in 1849. Groves thinks of Goethe's "mächtigen Felsen," found in *Wilhelm Meister's Years of Wandering*, as an erratic—an erratic conceived as a "mighty" rock.[4] Mighty in what sense, if not in the enchantment these rocks work upon us as we try to imagine their history? One gathers certain impressions or even affection for erratics. But what can one do with them? One might imagine collections of them as a kind of natural Zen garden. One might climb upon them, "boulder" upon them. One might imagine being like them.

As it happened, John Muir was described as "erratic" because he advocated leaving rocks alone. So reconsidered, that is just what California Congressman William Kent's declamation about Muir suggested: The end of the story is the rock where God put it. Muir used the term "erratic" only on rare occasions, and never for himself.

What is it to be among them? One often finds erratics upon *rôche moutonnées*, those rounded masses of rock, smoothed and striated by ice that has flowed over them. Well, they are not exactly rounded. A *rôche moutonnée* like Lembert Dome, which sits at the confluence of the Dana and Lyell forks of the Tuolumne River, is an outcrop of resistant bedrock with a gentle abraded slope on what would have been the upstream side of the ice (stoss slope) and a steep rougher slope on the downstream side (lee slope). Erratics perching on *rôche moutonnées* are personal favorites because of their surprising position and their aesthetic appeal—maybe they are even endearing, as Valerie says, because they're silly.

The obviously French name translates literally into English as "fleecy or sheep's wool rock," but is usually interpreted as meaning, rather unpoetically, "sheep rocks" or "sheepbacks." The term was first used in 1776 by the French geologist De Saussure; in 1883, another famous French geologist, M. de Lapparent, domesticated geology by saying that such rocks "produce an impression like that of a flock of sleeping sheep, hence the name *rôche moutonnée*." This can sometimes be quite a good description of them when seen from a distance.

The smooth upstream slope has been abraded by glacial ice exerting its full force as it flows up and over the rock, and the rough downstream "tail," or stoss, is due to the action of plucking, where ice has attacked the downstream side of the rock and literally pulled rock fragments away. "Plucking might occur as the ice moved up the stoss slope because there is a reduction in pressure, allowing liquid water to re-freeze and attach the ice to the underlying rocks."[5] All of this plucking is likely to supply some of the rocks that are fated to become erratics.

Ice does not polish granite surfaces; only rock polishes rock. So the smoothed, gentler and striated upstream slopes of a *rôche moutonnée*, scoured by the rock and gravel embedded in glacial ice, contrast with the steep, irregular, and jagged downstream slopes that have been plucked. Any mountain wanderer knows this and chooses a route through these sheep rocks accordingly. In Yosemite, we call these forms domes.

Generally speaking, one sits on a dome or a *rôche moutonnée* with pleasure, but on an erratic? Not so much. Many here are studded with feldspar crystals, making them pincushiony. If glacially polished granite is for walking upon, erratics are for stepping around. One also sits, usually on their upstream sides, which has the added advantage of yielding wider views of more elevated forms. There is also the matter of getting out of prevailing winds, which on a summer afternoon in

Tuolumne Meadows follow a direction opposite the historical glacial flow. Some of our favorite erratics perch immovably on some of our favorite domes. Others are to be found on glacial pavements in valleys, between domes.

In this light I must confess to being an inveterate trundler. To trundle is to cause a spherical or nearly spherical object to roll along. For mountaineers, trundling consists of rolling rocks, preferably over cliffs. My friend Tom Gerughty was a great trundler, and I remember an occasion when he put on a dramatic show of trundling at sunset in the Gorge of Despair, producing a show of sparks and the scent of ozone, which is the scent of fear for all climbers.

One can be overtaken against all judgment with the desire to trundle. I have been known to roll rocks in the wrong places, on the steep north slopes below Sentinel Rock and once high in the Hindu Kush. These memories give me shivers. My trundling behavior has always been associated with mixed feelings of joy and fear, but most of all with irresponsibility. After all, nobody who climbs mountains is unaware of the consequences of falling rocks. It is not the same to watch a rock fall as to make it fall. A good many people claim that they only trundle boulders and rocks to make climbing routes safe. This is unlikely to be their chief motive.

We had been doing it for years, calling it rock rolling, when the more formal term was introduced to one of my friends by the New Zealander Sir Edmund Hillary, who accomplished the first ascent of Mount Everest with Tenzing Norgay. He was also an enthusiastic trundler. Trundling, then, consists of rolling large rocks or boulders down mountains or cliffs, ravines and defiles. The practice can perhaps be traced back to eighteenth-century rock climbers in North America.

But of course modernizing trundling is absurd. Humans have been trundling for time far out of mind. Yet see how

S. F. Forrester, one early twentieth-century mountaineer, explains his behavior: "Boulder Trundling may be defined as the propulsion of fragments of the Earth's crust down mountain slopes of suitable inclination sooner than would occur from the interaction of natural forces."[6] The same author argues that Sisyphus is the first boulder trundler—who spent his whole life at it. But Leslie Stephen expresses the best and simplest case: "No one who cannot contentedly spend hours in that fascinating though simple sport really loves a mountain." Trundling must be part and parcel with the making of the Anthropocene.

To return to rocks in their set places: Erratics are not likely to move or fall unless a human moves them. One day in the Wind River Range, my father and I came upon a gigantic boulder, poised precariously, or so it seemed, on a ledge above a pass we were traversing as we entered the Cirque of the Towers. My father bet that I could not move that rock. I responded by climbing confidently up to the boulder and attempting to push it. I could not budge the boulder at all. Since that day, I have consistently tried to nudge boulders when I encountered them. On peaks above the flow of ancient glaciers, I have often found rocks amenable to rolling. But as for the boulders left by glaciers, the erratics—I have scarcely managed to move any of them. Sometimes I can make them rock in place, but more often they are immovable. I am not Sisyphus.

As for the interaction of natural and cultural forces—well that is my point. Erratics may not be icons for some people, and climbers often spend hours working out moves upon larger ones, doing something called bouldering. Erratics certainly have gained our respect, to the point that we might consider a trundler to be an iconoclast.

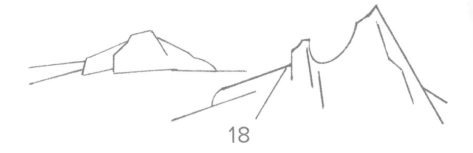

Iconic Landscape

Landmarks, large and small.

As Yosemite's National Park Service quite accurately claims, "The park boundary perfectly frames a landscape that is composed almost entirely of granite, and it's no surprise that this landscape contains some of the most iconic rock formations on Earth."[1]

We have come to take icons for granted, as if they are somehow apart from and immune from change. As with Yosemite at large, so with its parts. Recently a set of geologists wrote, "Tuolumne Meadows in Yosemite National Park is an iconic American landscape."[2] This place is iconic for cultural as well as natural reasons. For instance, here in 1889 John Muir and Robert Underwood Johnson began a journey down the Tuolumne River's canyon and planned what would become Yosemite National Park. Valerie and I and our infant son Jesse lived many summers almost precisely at the site where these talks commenced—lived there with marmots, flickers, bear, deer, coyotes, and an occasional badger or fisher in the midst of culturally and geologically iconic granite.

Representations of Yosemite mostly follow paradigms of geologists. Just so, Tuolumne Meadows, according to the premier early geologist of Yosemite, François Matthes, is the largest subalpine meadow in the Sierra Nevada.[3] Only more recently have some geologists considered Tuolumne Meadows to be a "geomorphic anomaly." As one article puts it, "this anomalous landscape is the result of preferential glacial erosion of highly fractured bedrock."[4]

An icon might be a picture, image, or other representation, often of some sacred personage, but more generally an icon functions as a sign or representation that stands for its object by virtue of a resemblance or analogy to it, as in semiotics. An icon might be a person or thing that is revered or idolized.

When a sign becomes an icon, it goes beyond arbitrary reference. An icon states a case and also embodies a case. Such are Yosemite's individual features and various landmarks: Half Dome, El Capitan, and Yosemite Falls. At large, Yosemite evolved as a national icon that embodies and stands for the nature and culture of California, for national parks, and finally for the greatness of United States. So be it.

In an important sense, an iconic landscape is *already* a representation; an iconic landscape is made of places that have been thoroughly iconized by literary and artistic representations. Like the Lake District in England, Yosemite Valley is weighted by an overload of representation—by the sheer quantity of elaborate, often repeated stereotypical depiction. No doubt Yosemite's landscapes reveal cultural clichés. Seen from the point of view of representation, these iconic landscapes are fetishizations, as Bill Cronon and others have noted. Mind you, it is not the region but the representations that fetishize Yosemite.[5] Yosemite is not a cliché but the experience of it might be.

In this strange way, what is represented becomes reversed, so that a visitor to Yosemite might focus primarily on what the representations of this place have to say about the culture that commodifies them. The actual region recedes from view; one loses one's sense of grounding. Tuolumne Meadows might be an iconic landscape, though not of the same weight as Yosemite Valley—and one can well ask, what does this region at the head of the Tuolumne River stand for? What cases do representations of these rocks make? Why are they revered? Is there any way to speak of this landscape without resorting to clichés about Edenic sites? This is and is not my question. While Tuolumne Meadows may be an iconic landscape, it differs from Yosemite Valley because the icons are so accessible and degraded too. Granted, much of the Tuolumne I witness and interact with is not very much like the "natural" or "wild" Tuolumne imagined of yore. Muir told Johnson that the Tuolumne watershed's biota had already been altered. The upper reaches of the Tuolumne were seasonally inhabited and crossed by aboriginal trading routes for probably two thousand years. Later, shepherds and miners followed these and, by the late nineteenth century, a road crossed the Sierra through Tuolumne Meadows.[6]

Now fishermen catch planted fish in the rivers, and as a result fewer frogs live here. The grazing of sheep in the last century permanently altered the biota; invasive species continue to arrive and flourish. The black bears have become domestic annoyances. As a result of misconceived road building that caused the photographer-conservationist Ansel Adams to explode in anger, the region now suffers from heavy auto and recreational vehicle traffic, illegal parking, mazes of footpaths, problems of sewage mismanagement, and water pollution.

Significant erosion creeps in a petty pace in shrinking meadows from day to day. Drought and forest management practices have engendered fires and alteration of the forests. Climate change has melted the glaciers. Drought has lengthened the dry seasons, so the impact of automotive visitors increases from year to year, particularly in the sensitive early season. After all, California's population has quadrupled in my lifetime. Without question, the global and the local interact in disturbing ways here. Let me clarify. I am willing to share

Tuolumne Meadows with an increasing number of visitors; they all arrive by auto, like us, but what is the cost?

We arrive via the modern Tioga Road, whose name is not native but an addition from mining interests. This highway now rarely follows native trails, and was pushed through the park by brute force. Never an attractive addition to the park, its narrow lanes are now choked by caravans of rented recreational vehicles and an increasing number of mobile homes as large as semi-trucks. An excessive number of visitors are only driving through, as if visiting Yosemite were primarily an automotive enterprise.

One can come to the granite of Tuolumne Meadows to think of these kinds of management issues. We are stubborn. Obstinately, what we care about here is radically local and no doubt myopic. As an environmental historian I go against the judgment of my peers. For instance, given "rapidly increasing connections around the globe," Ursula Heise writes, "what is crucial for ecological awareness and environmental ethics is arguably not so much a sense of place as a sense of planet," by which she means that "political, economic, technological, social, cultural, and ecological networks shape daily routines" and because "cultural practices become detached from place … these practices are now imbricated in such larger networks."[7]

I am sure that her closely reasoned perspective is correct, yet she also makes larger global networks iconic. This perspective is not, however, the light by which we or the community of friends who came together here chose our occupations; we have been largely driven by lifelong pursuit of the attachment of ad-hoc cultural practices to place. Heise accurately portrays Valerie's and my own ethical commitment when she notes that in the 1960s environmentalism acquired "an excessive investment in the local."[8] It is also true that we possess ambivalent views of the global. Though our past commitments to anti-war activities, justice for farm workers, and environmental justice still simmer, we now turn away from global issues and conundrums in our writing and painting to pursue in our work a "sense of place." I try to turn away, saying my commerce is with rock. Everyone needs a place. Our contribution to this premise—one that we all hold—should be clear by now.

Perhaps we have been privileged to be what some would call hobbyist environmentalists, but that is not all we do, and Valerie bristles at that phrase. We must also go outside and walk, ski, fish, draw, or even ride a bicycle for recreation. We would despair if we couldn't do these things, and think everyone ought to have a chance to get outside in a sometimes quiet, sometimes unpolluted, sometimes undisturbed place, where a person can use inherent biological senses. Also, we get angry when people mess up the granite of Yosemite by painting graffiti, building useless and damaging cairns, and creating unnecessary disturbances.

No modern person can claim to have local knowledge—because local knowledge is at root understood now as an anthropological notion about an indigenous community. What community we claim to speak for is not indigenous. We are not farmers here, nor hunters nor gatherers, though a couple we know did write a book entitled *Wild Food Plants of the Sierra*.[9] We can only claim to speak for what we find valuable. Perhaps this is a fantasy. If so, we have pursued it through all our years, and it is too late to change.

One has to be somewhere in one's mind. We choose to spend a lot of time in the mountains—even when not physically there—and find it helpful to be in a place, to do satisfactory things there. After our son's death, I wrote rather extensively about the disaster that occurs when someone is no longer located anywhere. We do claim to have had some nearly universal human experiences in places that matter. We might love to be more cosmopolitan, but not simply by a wider globetrotting.

Meanwhile, though in name a national park, Yosemite in practice has become an international park.[10] By 2009, the most recent study, 25% of its visitors were international. [11] Our own interests here in Tuolumne Meadows are and are not cosmopolitan. As literate citizens of a changing world, we are increasingly of this world, whether we wish to be or not. After all, we must own our own cosmopolitanism, if only because, as the sociologist Ulrich Beck reminds us, "The Nazis said 'Jew' and meant 'cosmopolitan'; the Stalinists said 'cosmopolitan' and meant 'Jew.'"[12]

We return to granite largely unaltered by human forces, draw near a legacy of what one geological report calls "a short-lived Cretaceous fracturing event associated with the Johnson Granite Porphyry's emplacement," and on our walks came to recognize decades ago the orientation, concentration, and distribution of "dense networks of sub-parallel opening-mode fractures that are clustered into discrete, tabular (book-like) zones" that constrained glacial erosion.[13] Like the geologists, we continue a tradition, representing the region surrounding Tuolumne Meadows in humanistic artistic terms as an interaction between the structure of a medium and a mode of erosion. Geomorphology, after all, consists of representation, but not just any representation will do. These forms will endure, just as the human desire to scramble on granite will.

The Sound of Talus

Can you run on broken rock?

THESE FORMS WILL endure but will not remain the same, because even granite fractures. When it breaks and begins to disassemble itself, for a while—a long while, beyond human senses of time—the assemblage may seem more like a jigsaw puzzle than like a chaos. But eventually things fall apart and become rubble. Talus, scree, debris.

Talus: This is what one calls piles of rocks that accumulate at bases of cliffs, chutes, or slopes, sitting at their angle of repose. *Talus* is a sort of quasi-geological term. Maybe it is a pile, and maybe it is a slope. If it is very unstable you might call it rubble, "rough, irregular stones broken from larger masses." One calls smaller debris *scree*; you can slide on it, sometimes pleasurably on descents, though not so much while ascending. The name *debris* connotes remains, waste, or rubbish that comes from breaking rocks.

It is hard to give order to this broken rock. The science writer James Gleick, most famous for his *Chaos: Making a New Science* (1987), believes that fractal relationships govern the scattering of rocks on a talus slope.[1] If so, the order is too sophisticated for me to see. In simple terms, when a talus slope accumulates, one looks up, recognizing a sign of instability. Talus is instability embodied. Traversing talus can be exhausting.

There is some disagreement about the value of talus or the importance of navigating it. In certain places, these rubble slopes extend for thousands of vertical feet. One wonders about the strange ambiguity in the etymology of this term *talus*, since it refers to both a bone in a human ankle and a slope on a mountain. That they should never meet! Talus can be an ankle-sprainer.

Muir could spiritualize a lesson of talus way beyond even Snyder's agile talus-hopper: "If for a moment you are inclined to regard these taluses as mere draggled, chaotic dumps, climb to the top of one of them, and run down without any haggling, puttering hesitation, boldly jumping from boulder to boulder with even speed. You will then find your feet playing a tune, and quickly discover the music and poetry of these magnificent rock piles—a fine lesson," he writes in *The Yosemite*. What could be less likely than human music played upon talus fields?

I certainly admit to anthropomorphizing rocks, but not in quite this way. It is hard to put a human face on talus. It is much easier to pick out mimetoliths, those rocks that look like humans or other living things.[2] Whenever humans imagine faces in rocks, these are not the true face of mountains. Even while I anthropomorphize, I firmly believe that when climbers speak of the faces of domes or mountains, these forms have no natural faces, music, or poetry. Rocks have no humanity, which is why I find them endlessly interesting.

Nevertheless, most humans have a tendency toward what David Hume called *pareidolia*, a universal tendency to imagine "all beings like themselves, and to transfer to every object those qualities with which they are familiarly acquainted;" as if there are "human faces in the moon" or "armies in the clouds," and especially to "ascribe malice and good will to everything that hurts or pleases us."[3] It is a pleasant entertainment to find music in talus, faces in rocks, bodies in clouds, flowers in snow crystals. As Molly Bloom would say, "Oh Rocks! . . . Tell us in plain words."

When Muir praised the music of talus, he must have had in mind old granite talus that has stabilized and settled, as you can recognize by the rounded corners of blocks and the lichen growing on their faces. Bearded talus is friendly, one might say. On the other hand, there is nothing quite like the fear that comes when one traverses new talus, smells ozone still in the air, and sees a patina of dust still coating the sharp-edged rocks, redolent of impact and friction. In my experience, volcanic talus never approaches the music and poetry Muir describes.

Talus bars ways to many worthwhile spaces unless one learns to get around on it. And getting around in the mountains is learned as surely as getting around in texts. Doug Robinson claims that "talus running is the bouldering of the mountaineer," an exercise that engages perception with motion. It is an activity to be sought out. For him, as for Gary Snyder, talus may seem like a sea of holes, in which case you must rise above them using balance, foresight, vision, and momentum.[4] It is easy to lose things between the boulders of a talus slope.

Some people refer to talus slopes as rock gardens. No doubt this is an ironic expression, since reasonable people agree with the many geologists who consider talus slopes dangerous terrain. After all, these fragments and boulders are sitting at their angle of repose. You may trigger a slide. In particular, as Robinson cautions, "beware of live moraines, they are pushed by insistently moving glaciers." It is hard for me to say what a live moraine might be, since they are kept in motion by either the advance or the retreat of a glacier. But true talus is not morainal, a moraine being an "irregular mass of unstratified glacial drift, chiefly boulders, gravel, sand, and clay" deposited and left on the ground by a glacier.

Some people distinguish between human-created talus gardens and moraine gardens, but they are speaking of landscapes humans build from stones, from talus and scree. For instance, according to David Sellars in *Rock Garden Quarterly,* "A scree slope can also be incorporated as part of the talus garden. However, the surfaces of talus and moraine deposits are varied with dips, hollows, pools, and small cliffs, leaving plenty of latitude for creativity."[5]

To return to so-called "natural rock gardens," according to advice found in diverse places on the web, there is no geological information to be gained from walking on scree. This seems to be not entirely true. For instance, it is apparent that some sorting occurs in scree as in talus. Surely this is, in itself, informative.

One can gather more subjective impressions if not geological information. One might encounter both good and bad rubble. For instance, in those rare places where talus lies under snowfields for much of the year, water tinkling under the snow eventually readjusts these rocks, quiets them so that they lie down like cobblestones, fitting them to each other. These are Valerie's favorite places. Good rubble, then, is the kind of rubble one might like to create, if only one could. There is such a place on the way to Matthes Crest, and there are other examples elsewhere in the region. The result is something not at all like sliding on loose scree, or tripping on unstable talus—rocks so neatly cobbled that, naturally, we admire them, especially when they sit above braided streams of snowmelt.

The fortunate aspect of Tuolumne Meadows is that the glaciers swept most of the talus away. In many places, but not all, one sidles up smooth slaps to the unperturbed peaks. On the other hand, just to the east, one enters a world of interminable talus. While ascending unbroken rock can be a pleasure one hopes will never end, ascending talus is a project where one hopes for the end. The mountains contradict themselves and contain multitudes. What is now a silent pile of talus was once a fall of rock.

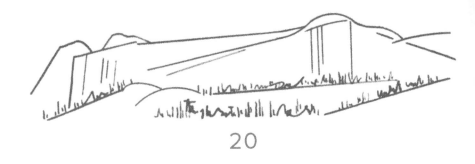

Fairview Dome

We consider the proliferation of domes.

As its name suggests, Fairview Dome is valued as a viewpoint. "At first sight it seems inaccessible, though a good climber will find it may be scaled on the south side," as Muir writes. In fact, well into middle age, my mother once walked up the southern backside with a group led by a park interpreter to what Muir called its "burnished crown" and perhaps even following his advice in *The Yosemite*:

> About half-way up you will find it so steep that there is danger of slipping, but feldspar crystals, two or three inches long, of which the rock is full, having offered greater resistance to atmospheric erosion than the mass of the rock in which they are imbedded, have been brought into slight relief in some places, roughening the surface here and there, and affording helping footholds.[1]

Some people describe it as a sugarloaf-shaped dome. Its structure is more complicated and elegant than that. Probably Fairview is the archetypal dome of Tuolumne Meadows, though at one point Muir refers to its form as that of a "hard residual knot . . . an illustration of the survival of the strongest and most favorably situated." The shape and surfaces combine to render this rock monolithic—all of one piece.

Its base is easily accessible from the Tioga Road, though most visitors drive right by it. According the USGS

"Geographical Names System," it is about two miles north of Cathedral Peak and four miles west of Tuolumne Meadows. As Grove Karl Gilbert described it as part of a classic essay on mountain sculpture in 1904, Fairview stands at the edge of a plateau, its summit eight hundred feet above one base and thirteen hundred feet above the other: "though not above timber-line, [it] is bare of trees, because in the absence of joints they get no foothold."[2] This is not entirely true. There are a few pines growing near the summit.

This landmark has gone by the names Glacier Monument, Soda Springs Dome, Soda Springs Butte or Buttes, Tuolumne Glacier Monument, or Tuolumne Monument.[3] As these names suggest, Fairview Dome is a major landmark in Tuolumne meadows. At an elevation of 9,714 feet (2,961 meters), its summit provides wide and general views of the region and, in turn, it is widely and generally visible from many portions of the region. You can see it from the grocery store.

What is Fairview Dome? Certainly it is no boulder, though Muir thought it might have seemed so to the Tuolumne glacier. Consequently, Muir named it "Tuolumne Glacier Monument, one of the most striking and best preserved of the domes." Like other domes in Tuolumne, it has a few erratics "nicely poised on its crown," as Muir put it. It is made entirely of Cathedral Peak Granodiorite. Though prominent, it is one of many well-preserved domes.

Fairview sits in the midst of many striking granite forms that reveal themselves along the Tioga Road as a driver leaves Tenaya Lake. The road follows a weakness in the batholith as one heads north, leaving the Half Dome Granodiorite of Polly Dome and Tenaya Peak, which is barely distinguishable from the Cathedral Peak Granodiorite that one enters and that makes up Pywiack, Medlicott, Daff, Fairview, and several other less prominent domes. Almost certainly, it follows the route of original inhabitants of the region. Over about five miles of driving, many domes appear to the right and left as one heads toward a small divide that leads to Tuolumne Meadows. These were all mantled with ice when the main arm of Tenaya Canyon's glacier began its descent.

What is a dome and why? Though not usually symmetrical, why are they so rounded? Gilbert uses Fairview Dome as an exemplar of dome structure, noting "curved plates or sheets which wrap around the topographical forms," and he posits various possible causes for this unique form.[4] As he argues, there must be some relation between structure and form. He considers three possible causes: secular changes in temperature, but not annual and diurnal changes because their influence penetrates only a small distance; expansive force developed in weathering; and what he calls "dilation from unloading," or release of compressive stress created as the intrusive granite cooled, of which he has "no direct knowledge." This last one, he finds, is the most likely explanation for their "rounding."

Rock climbers are particularly attracted to Fairview Dome's north and west wall—and Medlicott's and Pywiack's west walls. When I was young, we took these impressive cliffs for a playground, a gymnasium. During Valerie's and my fifty years in Tuolumne, climbers developed dozens of routes up the steep and polished north, northwest, and west sides of these and other rounded domes. These entailed precise, minute, and exacting inspections of these and other faces of rock, pursued for some decades. Some of the routes on Fairview are nearly a thousand vertical feet in length, and several of them are considered "classic climbs." The first was ascended in 1958. Like many of my climbing companions, I have been up maybe a half dozen of them, several of them repeatedly. Now we frequently walk around the base, admiring.

The south, or what Muir calls the backside, of Fairview is not where the hard climbing resides. For climbers, the shadowed northwest side offers sites for many heroic accomplishments. Here are found some of the most challenging routes of the region on steep polished rock. It can be intimidating. The feldspar crystals Muir admires were honed down on the north and east side by glaciers, often pared down to small edges. Unlike the original classic route, the western smooth steep walls require moving up almost featureless areas. One uses the edges of golden plates of polish a great deal on these faces. In places the rock seems almost glasslike in its sheen. Early on a cool morning the rock on the northeast face seems particularly inhospitable, cold, smooth, and greasy feeling. Somehow Cathedral Peak Granodiorite becomes more resistant, more unyielding here. Further to the south, where the routes are shorter, feldspar pops out of the surfaces; the rock has more features and is not so steep.

Jay Taylor documents the development in Yosemite of the climber's "topo," a graphic form of climbing guide, that evolved from simple line drawings (see figure 20.1). "By the mid-1970s climbers had a standardized topo lexicon, thus solving many of the problems inherent in verbal descriptions." These "topos" became guides, and in Yosemite Valley, particularly, as he argues, "topos" reveal "a multiplicity of social spaces, intertwined and simultaneous yet independent. Accessing these landscapes necessitates moving across texts, from state and NGO reports to native stories, nature writings, tourist brochures, and the spatial information left by recreationists."[5] In fact, I rarely used these line drawings, but depended primarily on verbal descriptions.

Whatever internal forces shaped Fairview, Medlicott, and Pywiack domes, glaciers influenced where these steep walls are and how they are finished. According to Craig H. Jones, "The

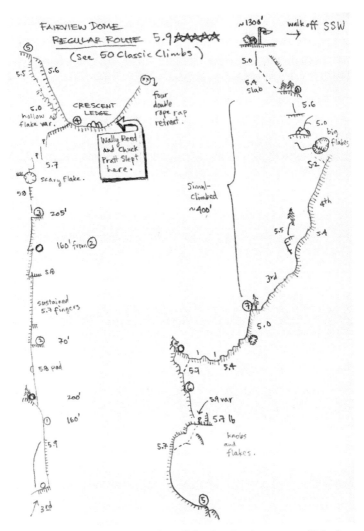

FIGURE 20.1. This is a typical "topo" for the classic route on Fairview Dome. Source: Courtesy of Robert Hanson: https://www.math .utah.edu/~bobby/climbing/tuolumne/fairviewtopo.jpg

Tuolumne glacier traversed an area with the youngest granites of the Sierra, and these are generally unfractured."[6] Further, because the Grand Canyon of the Tuolumne was V-shaped, it restricted the flow of ice from Muir's *mer de glace* and "the result was that the ice so filled the basin that it poured over the divide into Tenaya Creek and down into the more easily eroded rocks of the Yosemite Valley."[7]

There are disagreements about this matter, as another set of geoscientists attribute the proliferation of domes to "variable glacial erosion due to the presence or absence of pre-existing bedrock fractures." They account for the meadows and valleys through locally pervasive "concentrated tabular fracture clusters" particularly susceptible to glacial erosion in the granitic bedrock. "We propose that Tuolumne Meadows proper exemplifies a case where ice flow was perpendicular to closely spaced fractures."[8]

Nevertheless, a sizable portion of the glacier's force turned south—though of course glaciers do not turn—smoothing and polishing the unfractured rock of these domes. The stunning shape and finish of the northwest or west walls of Medlicott and Fairview domes (and even a small portion of Pywiack's east wall) are remarkably similar, which is not simply because of their type of granodiorite.

On one level, I want to say that only when you climb on this rock—where you must trust feldspar to hold onto, and where you must closely scrutinize its surfaces to spot where glacial polish has chipped for edges that provide footholds—only then can you really know what granite is or can be for any person. But there are no doubt higher uses for such a well-finished landform than viewing or climbing—and maybe the highest use was developed by Grove Karl Gilbert as he tried to understand what is so aesthetically striking about these forms. During several seasons, including 2017, the Park Service closed a few climbing routes on Fairview and Medlicott domes in early summer to accommodate pairs of breeding peregrine falcons who nested on the steepest western side of the orange-tinted cliffs.

Birds of prey need not fear our passing. We walk pleasantly over, around, and through the crevices and valleys between these bosses of polished rock, among the steep faces and gently sloping sides of these domes, and have done so every summer for most of our lives. Sometimes we stop at places called Lake of the Domes, Cathedral Lakes, or Polly Dome Lakes. The possible walks seem endless, though they are not. Sameness and difference in the surfaces of the rocks determine where one can step confidently and where not. Though geologists attempt to render historical the shapes of these forms, these rocky places defy explanation without the scale of the dynamic human body. They seem almost mythical in their reality until touched, granitic mazes with neither entirely accessible nor inaccessible passages, sometimes marked by hikers, climbers, even ourselves, where one might get lost but never does.

Above and Below:
Ghosts of Glaciers

I go to Cathedral Peak to consider glacial polish.

CONSIDERING THAT THE glaciated world is already sufficiently composed, we sometimes wish to explore a few modes of getting above it. From above, there seems nothing tumultuous about what has been glaciated, nothing disturbed or excited here. It is as if forces of the world were in remission. These valleys and canyons below seem pure and smooth, impermeable, exacting in their permanence. Glacial pavements, their surfaces devoid of soil. Down below, one can sit almost anywhere comfortably. An occasional glacial erratic, stranded when ice melted out from under it. Glacial lakes. Like me, if only I could be myself. And then one looks closer. Yes. Bedrock appears up high in the Sierra Nevada where we like to go. Bedrock shaped by glaciers is best seen in places like Tuolumne Meadows. Here one treads upon the foundation of the Sierra.

The mirror sharpness of glacially carved granite, of bare naked rock, reflects more than one human desire. Above glacial history, the rock reveals a far different face, more austere, easier to ascend, less comfortable for sitting. Granite meets a different desire here. Through much of the Tuolumne region, this unglaciated granite has weathered into a variegated and, as some geologists put it, a coarsened texture. I care about the formal qualities of these high granite forms because of

the many ways they resist and yet allow a person to wander
silently among their glistening shapes. The rock up high is
rougher stuff.

Climbing Cathedral Peak is such an obvious thing to do because it is so central to geological and cultural histories of
Tuolumne Meadows. Even the longest climbing route on its
southeast side, first ascended at about the time I was born, is
considered these days to be a "moderate" rock climb and is
heavily populated.

Perhaps it should be named Feldspar Peak since these crystals—in geologist's terms "megacrysts of K-feldspar"—give a
unique character to the climbing; their profusion seems the
same all around. Also, because of a high proportion of quartz,
Cathedral Peak has a tendency to sparkle.[1]

These so-called "microcline megacrysts in the Cathedral
Peak Granodiorite" came about by "textural coarsening
(Ostwald Ripening) of earlier formed crystals" that "nucleated
and grew in an environment of increasing undercooling, probably during the ascent of the magma." Some dissolved in the
interstitial melt, but the larger ones grew. Especially feldspar
grew, and these structures are more resistant to weathering.[2]

During most of my summers in the Sierra, I visited this
route's nubbled granite and over many years approached the
summit from all four cardinal directions. I no longer remember how many times. I ascended its most popular routes with
friends, with Valerie before and after we were married, with my
son Jesse, and with students; I guided strangers on it a couple
of times. Sometimes I went alone. I do not get excited about
Cathedral Peak really: It is more like being with an old friend.

Almost all approaches to this peak are in themselves pleasant. I especially enjoy an approach from the north, passing

Fairview Dome on my right and continuing up the gently ascending north ridge. For the most part, climbing on Cathedral Peak granite is straightforward because of protruding feldspar crystals that have remained after surrounding minerals have weathered away. Many of these grow as big as a human fist. Climbing on this kind of granite is sometimes called knob climbing. This mountain is full of possibilities, so many that one might almost say there is no best route. But like others who go to this peak regularly, I have my favorite spots, stances, and even handholds.

Cathedral Peak's granite may be about eighty-eight million years old, and it is heavily weathered. Because of these feldspar crystals you can go almost anywhere here if you are careful and know what you are doing. Although the summit ridge looks all pinnacled from below, up high it seems more like an assortment of slightly teetering blocks. I have never seen a large block move here. Perhaps it is only us, the climbers, who teeter.

Approaching the summits—there are two summits to Cathedral Peak—gives a full appreciation for the actual footprint of this strangely transverse double peak. The lower but more imposing west summit is named Eichorn Pinnacle, for the famous climber Jules Eichorn. Its west ridge or pillar, as it is sometimes called, affords somewhat more challenging climbing, steeper where the feldspar-studded rock shows less relief and climbing becomes more difficult.

Cathedral Peak, Echo Peaks, Cockscomb, and Matthes Crest intrude doubly into the sky. They are known as nunataks or, to be more precise, former nunataks—the name for islands that rose above glaciers and were never covered. These ridges, towers, and pinnacles studded with protruding feldspar crystals mark boundaries and borders of a glacial past.

One of our favorite outings wanders around these nunataks surrounding Budd Lake, between Cathedral Peak and

Echo Peaks, along the edge and overlooking the west aspect of Matthes Crest. Sometimes we descend to Cathedral Lake, circumnavigating Cathedral Peak. Sometimes I undertake a longer circuit, circumnavigating Matthes Crest.

Meandering Around Matthes Crest

A walk around a hidden landmark.

LIKE MANY OTHERS, I was schooled in geological time by the idealistic paintings on the wall of the old Yosemite Museum— dark oils, each image a scene of early morning when northwest slopes were shadowed. There is a certain roundness and gentleness to these imaginary landscapes. Made by Herbert A Collins Jr. and Sr. under the supervision of François Emile Matthes, they iconize a history of Yosemite landmarks in six steps: broad valley stage, mountain valley stage, canyon stage, and glacial stages leading to our own post-glacial era. The paintings at the Yosemite Museum taught that we, the inheritors of the Yosemite landscape, stand at the end of a placid geo-scientific and artistic history. We return to these images though we know now that there is no end to Yosemite's natural and cultural history.

As a child, I was especially drawn by the glacial stages Collins imagined. Then, as Matthes wrote, the northern uplands, the Tuolumne regions, were "mantled in ice." Caped, covered, shrouded, before shapes of the present that would become my world emerged into blazing sunlight. Though I now know from considerable experience that glaciers are neither placid nor particularly attractive aesthetically, I was captivated at the time by these images. They predicted my early experiences in the Tuolumne region long before I visited the high country.

Off in the distant left-hand corner of those illustrative paintings, a narrow crest of rock reaches out from the Cathedral Range, jutting almost due south, as if it were a microcosm of the range of light. It rose barely above ice of the glacial world. Now its steep flanks rise out of gentle valleys, graced on each side by lakes. Now it is possible to contemplate the crest from below, to amble about it as if it were a sculpture, while examining multiple symmetries from eastern and western perspectives. Indeed, its flanks rise steeply, about a thousand feet above Echo Lake on the west or Matthes Lake on the east. The lakes themselves are close to the headwaters of Cathedral Fork of Echo Creek, which joins the Merced River a mile or so above Moraine Dome. It is rare to meet a mountain in the Sierra Nevada that has an impressive face on both the east and west sides.

Where did the rock surrounding this narrow crest go? Well known as an interpreter of Yosemite glacial history, Grove Karl Gilbert stood about a hundred years ago down near the Merced, his right hand on a huge erratic boulder made of Cathedral Peak Granite, which rested on a pedestal. I like to imagine that piece of Cathedral Peak Granite—so obvious by the studding of big feldspar crystals that project from its surface—making its own unfinished journey, perhaps even from the drainage of the Tuolumne River when the Tuolumne *mer de glace* overflowed to the south. Or perhaps Gilbert's boulder was quarried by a glacier from the side of Matthes Crest. Such an event, below the surface of the present, is invisible in the Collins' paintings.

On the map of Yosemite, one looks above and to the right of Yosemite Valley. On the ground you have to go looking for the Matthes Crest; you cannot see it from the usual viewpoints.

This is a question of lighting in part. When you get up high it sometimes appears as a striking dramatic form, blazing white in the sun, but on cloudy days the crest seems to fade into the bare bones of the region, being only one small part of a vast collection of exposed granite ribs that punctuate the domes and peaks.

This present landmark, a fin or blade of granite, was not always called the Matthes Crest, but acquired its distinctive reputation from more recent writers. In 1949 for instance, when I was five years old, one Sierra Club journalist said it was "perhaps the most spectacular cockscomb in the Cathedral Range . . . a knifelike ridge south of the Echo Peaks, which has remained virtually unknown," never officially named, but often called "Echo Ridge."[1] This writer, Reid V. Moran, also observed that its most inspiring aspect was from the southeast, from what is now called Matthes Lake, where there are no established trails.

Sometimes it seems an anomaly in the landscape. From the right perspective—particularly that of rock climbers who like bold and manly comparisons—it is a knife edge, a serrated white cleaver, great and wondrous. A more analytical view suggests a three-part structure. The southern section is marked, as Moran noticed in 1949, by a "curiously arched jointing of the granite," the middle section is an obelisk, and the northern section a short notched ridge.

This landmark spoke to geologists and informed both their description and their histories of the landscape. Matthes himself struggled to fashion a proper language for describing such a place or landmark. In *The Incomparable Valley*, he wrote, it "formerly rose as an island (*nunatak*) from the icefield that overswept the Tuolumne-Merced Divide."

In his original essay of 1920, "Cockscomb Crest," Matthes noted that the term *nunatak* is Eskimo (or Inuit, as modern writers would say), borrowed by physiographers from the in-habitants of Greenland and used as a technical term for rocky summits arising above surrounding ice sheets and glaciers. As he said, "The pinnacles and crests of the Cathedral Range might, therefore, be referred to as former *nunataks.* But the ap-propriateness and desirability of so styling them are, in the writ-er's opinion, open to question." He had quite a lot to say about this ridge later named for him, but he refers to it as Echo Crest.[2]

Why open to question? Because other portions of the Sierra remained above ice, and yet are not so distinctive as landforms or landmarks. Also, Matthes wanted "a distinctive term for the more fragile, evanescent forms" of the present landscape he was describing. He needed a name not for the glacial land-scape in the painting that so entranced my younger self, but for the modern landscape that we enter when we behold granite forms of Yosemite.

Indeed Matthes was possessed by the question of proper names. In his own self-deprecating and slightly humorous way, he decided on the term "Cockscomb." Now the peak that he named "Cockscomb" is still labeled as such on modern maps: "seen endwise, it seems but a narrow blade, springing almost without transition from the broad mountain under it," as he had written. Yet, as he also observed, "from certain directions it is suggestive of the upper half of an ornamental 'fleur-de-lis,' but from most viewpoints it resembles nothing so much as a splendidly sculptured, gigantic cockscomb."

Matthes suspected that something was amiss with his com-parison, perhaps because it suggested something of the small pride of roosters, or perhaps because it was demeaned by its association with barnyard birds. "The writer does not claim to be a connoisseur in poultry," he commented wryly, but the likeness was "as close as one might expect to find in a piece of mountain sculpture."[3]

With this crest now named for him, Matthes was a pioneer in two ways. He wanted to understand the landmarks of the region, but also wished to meet "the duty before us," as he called it, to name and speak justly of these forms. Writing began for him with the desire of "finding suitable names for the features of the High Sierra."[4]

The landmark we call Matthes Crest is more monumental than a cockscomb: a mile and a half long of jagged granite, it seems like an unfinished work, each segment grained at a different angle, juxtaposed, and fused to the next as if assembled incompletely by a master of parquetry. Or else we might imagine it disassembled incompletely by time. The crest does not dominate the landscape so much as it informs the region. Apart from the pure pleasure of traveling here, I have been hanging around it these many years in hopes that I might be informed.

One irresistible journey follows the paths of the glaciers that worked the granite of this ridge. How much they worked it is a matter of continuing debate. This saunter around Matthes Crest reveals a small portion of the Cathedral Range. I might call such an exercise a circumambulation, but the journey around Matthes Crest is not a circle—more like a meander. The virtue of this itinerary is that it departs from the trails but is not a difficult enterprise. Walking around the Matthes Crest is an exercise in following the shapes of glacial geology in no particular hurry, with no particular goal.

I begin in Tuolumne Meadows where the Tuolumne ice field or *mer de glace* itself flowed and overleapt the Cathedral Range. I ascend Budd Creek, cross the Cathedral Range at Echo Peaks, drop into the drainage east of the Matthes Crest, descend the broad valley to Matthes Lake, then skirt the south edge of the crest and ascend to Echo Lake, where I often pause for a swim and test the aptness of this lake's name before returning in late afternoon along the western face of the Echo

Peaks, traversing a set of well-placed grassy benches and descending Budd Creek to Tuolumne Meadows. There are more than two perspectives on this daylong mountain ramble, and on this day I come close to all of Matthes's favorite crests.

About forty years ago, I would race with a friend to the south edge of the Matthes Crest and traverse the very spine of it from south to north, a long but relatively easy rock climb for the Tuolumne region. I believe that doing this climb a couple times taught me something about other lines of approach to the region because the climb itself is a traverse. Other days, climbers of my generation would scramble to the summits of Tenaya Peak, the Echo Peaks, Columbia Finger, the Cockscomb, Tressider Peak, Eichorn Pinnacle, Unicorn Peak, and Cathedral Peak. We took these climbs as diversions from the more difficult ascents in the region.

There was a time—before I became a climber—when reaching the summit of the Matthes Crest was considered a daunting task. According to some historians, in 1931 the proper modern use of the climbing rope was introduced to the Sierra Club by Francis P. Farquhar and Robert L. M. Underhill. As a result, on July 26, Glen Dawson, Walter Brehm, and Jules Eichorn reached the highest point of what was then called "Echo Ridge," ascending from the east. In June 1947, Chuck and Ellen Wilts accomplished the first traverse of the arête from the south to the summit.

Matthes Crest is not like most of the routes climbed most frequently in the region these days. It is relatively far from the road, taking over two hours of pretty fast striding to approach. The rock itself is typical of the region, studded with feldspar. But the Matthes Crest offers much easier climbing than the mirror-smooth flanks of domes like Fairview because it is all chunky along the crest, full of handholds and footholds. (Of course—this ridge-top was not polished and smoothed by the glacier.)

One sometimes climbs along the very crest, experiencing great exposure on both sides. Sometimes one traverses around small pinnacles on the west or east, and sometimes one must drop into fissures or gaps where the grain of the rock changes direction.

There is nothing smooth about this traverse until, toward the end, all difficulties cease and one coils the rope. Then there is a great relief and pleasure to finish along a rough, broad, flat expanse of slightly pink slabs that reach over half a mile toward the Cathedral Range. Although there is a summit somewhere behind, one passed it as if it were only another turret, as part of the traverse. There is no obvious crux pitch on this climb, and nothing seems so important or so pleasing as the final stroll across these slabs.

It is all a question of perspective. You can and cannot see the Matthes Crest while climbing on it, and so, too, you can and cannot see it from below. Climbing on it one learns with hands and feet the very texture and feel of this crystalline rock. Walking round it, as Matthes did, gives a broader sense of the shape and architecture of this region, but maybe I get so much pleasure hanging around the base of Matthes Crest because I have traversed its summit ridge.

Now, I jaunt, stroll, amble, wander—call it what you will. I am out and about, engaged with the rock. Sometimes, during such days, I sense that this is the most complete thing I have ever done; beautiful in the way my body moves through the larger body of a world I can trust. The rhythm of steps, the resilience of the Earth in its hard places and soft, the very contours of the pavements and bogs, the way the canyons and ridges seem to open up in all directions: Whatever transpires is like a deep pure breath, cold and like the mythological petrified ice that cuts to the center of my being, filling it with light.

I remember this whenever I pass the southeast buttress of Cathedral Peak, and hear climbers speaking or shouting to each other. An urgency in their voices sticks to my senses and makes me a little nervous. It is as if I am returned to a past when climbing was my chief activity here.

My own changes of perspective suggest that the crest—the Sierra itself—is open to multiple interpretations. What one learns of it depends on one's expectations. Although great sermons have been written about walking, its benefits have become, for me, a kind of business as usual, only more so.

Sometimes, for instance, one comes upon a unique geographical feature that the map does not even suggest. One day Valerie and I came upon such a place: the wonderful meadowed ledges under the western face of the Echo Peaks. These ledges are part of the grain that one would intuit while inspecting the shapes of the region—no surprise to a walker, though absent from the map. What we thought, immediately, was that these ledges would be a perfect location for a camp. The next time we passed by, the meadow was a bog and the air was thick with mosquitoes. We had to run away.

Often these places of human fantasy or intuition become distractions and lead away from the smooth route drawn on the map. Complex grains or crusts of these ridges are most interesting when one follows their crests, but some ridges lead away from a planned itinerary, to soft places where one wishes only to sit, rest, contemplate, and snack.

Flowers, too, are always a distraction. When my parents, for instance, would say they were going for a hike, I would wonder why they spent all their time sitting by the wayside, pleased to identify or contemplate a particular flower. I myself enjoy the flowers, but usually from a certain distance and at a certain speed, as I go by them. I do not sit down much to dine on them. I am not, as Valerie says, much of a "flower glutton," not yet. She, however, draws and paints the Sierra's flowers and trees.

When you cross the Cathedral Range, you are truly away from the Tioga Road. The Matthes Crest, so near and so accessible, lies almost hidden from the realm of automotive Yosemite. It is a nearby yet distant portion of an easily accessible backcountry. From many places the Tioga Road is barely visible, and from some, it is audible as well. But down the east side of Matthes Crest, the morning sun in one's face, the wall lit up like a sheet of fire, the landscape seems like it might be far away.

There are almost always new signs of black bear at Matthes Lake. I never see one and only briefly wonder what they have been doing here. Then I turn the corner, enter a different drainage, and forget the bears while deciding whether I will contour around through a field of talus or drop down into Echo Creek and then follow the creek back upstream. I choose the slightly longer route in the meadows by the creekside.

I have come down what I think of as Matthes Creek in the driest of years when I crunched through a good deal of coarse sand, and in the wettest of years I slogged through snowfields on the north side of the Cathedral Range. In the past I have camped in several places along the way, at Budd Lake when that was permitted, at Matthes Lake, and at the Cathedral Lakes. Now I think this region ought to be day-hiking country for the good of the land, and because in some places it is better to be passing through.

But on a hot summer day, it is impossible not to linger by a lake and take a dip. Probably Budd Lake is the choicest swimming lake of the three I pass, but Echo Lake appears at about the time one is most ready to strip off clothes, dive into cold water, and sun-dry, tingling on a warm white rock. Nobody I know who has spent any time in the region has failed to jump into Budd Lake naked. I was reminded of this the last time we passed by, when we saw a girl striding sprightly around the other side of the lake. She stopped and undid her hair, and we knew what was coming next. Off went her clothes and she leapt into the water, feet first, one arm outstretched. When we left she was nude on a warm rock.

It may well be that the chief wonder in the Tuolumne region comes from texture, shape, and flow of rock, soil, and water under foot—the sharp contrasts of textures from bright variegated granite to transparent quartz, to opaque, knobbed, rough feldspar-studded Cathedral Peak granite that dominates the bedrock, to the heavy sand of the decomposed granite, littered by detached feldspar crystals, gradually flowing and sifting down to bogs and marshes, ponds and creeks.

On saddles and crests of the ridges in this region there are often potholes or "weather pans," as geologists call them: round, flat-bottomed depressions that are sometimes filled with sand in which the incompletely decomposed chips of feldspar sit like a carefully arranged mosaic. They are like miniature illustrations of the larger processes at work here.

Matthes called them weathering pits: "the development of cavities of this type" where "a small initial hollow having been formed by the decomposition . . . becomes a receptacle for water from rains or melting snow and is enlarged gradually by both chemical and mechanical processes." He also noticed that weather pits do not occur on freshly glaciated rock surfaces. He found not a single one within the area that was covered by the later glaciers.[5] Consequently, weathering pits, with their overhanging rims, show long exposure to weather since glaciation.

According to N. King Huber, weathering commonly enlarges small natural depressions on surfaces where water collects; he has no certain explanation for the fact that they are typically flat-bottomed but proposes that "the margins tend to deepen and enlarge until all points of the bottom of the pan are equally wet or dry at the same time. Thereafter, they weather downward at a rate that is constant over all of the pan surface." Surely the process is slow, since "such pans normally are not found on surfaces scraped smooth during the last major glaciation, which ended some 10,000 years ago."[6]

I may focus on the wonderful clarity of the water of the Sierra, the crisp contrast of the white chunks of snow still floating in a newly melted-out lake. And how cold it feels when it envelops my body. Or it may be the air, so palpable when one comes out of a Sierra lake, tingling and alive, the skin awake to the least breath of wind. And the air all around, sometimes filled with mosquitoes, as it was that day when we hurried across those ledges west of Echo Peaks. There is very little human pleasure outside the body, but the human body is, thankfully, semipermeable.

One descends granite and gravel in the drainage that feeds Matthes Lake to the soft and lumpy alpine meadows surrounding it. Early in some seasons, these are filled with shooting stars.

What is happening to Matthes Lake, to the gullies that face Budd Lake, to the flowers, to the timberline trees near the crest of the Cathedral Range? What is happening to the trail up Budd Creek? To the climbers? What is happening to the time? Or to me as I complete this circuit once again? As I write this, nothing much is happening to the Matthes Crest, and everything is happening around it. Probably nothing will change its skyline during the human occupation of this planet. This leads many people I know to think that the Tuolumne region is the still center of the universe. This granite rib is a still point, a central topographical fact. But where I put my feet, things change from year to year, and during various times of the year. Remembering and forgetting, I change too.

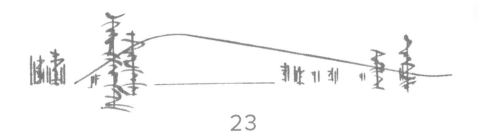

The View
from Pothole Dome

What is a dome and what can you see there?

FROM PARTS OF OUR journeys around Cathedral Crest we can look back toward the west end of Tuolumne Meadows marked by Pothole Dome, gently sloping, easily approachable, with panoramic views; a peaceful summit planted with lodgepole pines, and therefore appropriate for a wedding party. Valerie and I were married here in June 1968. We return every year and learn more about this place and ourselves each time.

Pothole Dome is generally taken to be a typical *rôche moutonnée*. Belying its placid appearance from afar, glacial inscriptions on its surface reveal a very elaborate structure and a turbulent history. This scalloped, low-lying hump that signals an end of Tuolumne Meadows proper and a beginning of the river's canyon has features more complex than the striated lines on its smooth glacial polish that reveal the direction of the glacier's flow.

Along the way you can inspect occasional chatter marks, little crescent gouges from rocks dragged by glacial ice. Its summit and slopes are littered with interesting erratics. Most obviously, Pothole Dome is named for potholes and flutes created by turbulent fast-flowing rivers from the past. These potholes themselves were eroded beneath the glacier and many of them still retain their grinding stones. Apparently, water from the surface of the glacier fell down vertical shafts called *moulins* and then flowed underneath the ice.

Grove Karl Gilbert was uncharacteristically uncertain when he viewed these *moulins* or glacial mills, as he called them:

> [I] encountered an aberrant and puzzling type of sculpture. Inclined surfaces, so situated that they can not have been subjected to postglacial stream scour, are sometimes carved in a succession of shallow, spoon-shaped hollows, and at the same time are highly polished. They resemble to a certain extent the surfaces sometimes wrought by glaciers on well-jointed rocks, where the hackly character produced by the removal of angular blocks is modified by abrasion; but they are essentially different.[1]

Though their "hackly character" was erased, they lacked the signs of glacial finishing.

A *moulin* is by definition "a narrow, tubular chute or crevasse through which water enters a glacier from the surface." And one sometimes sees giant kettles or potholes that were formed at the bottoms of moulins by rocks and boulders transported by falling water.[2]

Finally, flutes are those visible, smooth, deep, gutter-like channels formed on the scour, stoss, or uphill side (as opposed to the pluck side) of the dome. On Pothole Dome, these indicate that water flowed uphill over the dome, as what Muir called the Tuolumne *mer de glace* descended into its canyon.[3]

When one is on Pothole Dome, one is under flowing waters of the past, under Muir's ancient Tuolumne River *mer de glace*. We can imagine, if we wish, that we are under a sea of ice here, where water is and is not petrified, glacial ice being made of crystals under great pressure that move in what is called plastic flow. We are not in danger of being dragged along, eroded, or ground up.

Yet with such signs of turbulence, Pothole Dome might be taken as an emblem of our own fifty-year history together. It has become, for us, another center of the known world, our own humble *axis mundi*. It marks a change, where the placid river plunges toward a descent into cascades: Tuolumne Falls, White Cascade, California, LeConte, Waterwheel Falls, and eventually the Grand Canyon of the Tuolumne. Sometimes, we turn west toward what we call our dome walk.

We proceed due north, over the top of Pothole Dome, to take in the view of Mount Conness, Matterhorn Peak, Whorl Mountain, the rim of peaks near the northern edge of the Tuolumne Intrusive Suite. These glacial peaks rise above their glacial past. We recede into memories of traveling in this northern high country.

The skyline above glaciers of the past always seems another slightly dreamy world. Even when climbing in Yosemite Valley, say on El Capitan, there is a substantial demarcation from slick lower walls to the huge dihedrals of unglaciated rock above. Climbing El Cap seems, in some sense, like proceeding from one monolith to another. But to return to Tuolumne.

Mount Conness dominates the north because it is so close, so central, and so prominent. Clarence King, who first ascended it, speaks of "that firm peak with titan strength and brow so square and solid, it seems altogether natural we should have named it for California's statesman, John Conness."[4] It was named by the Whitney Survey for the remarkable senator from California (1821–1909). Conness introduced the bill in 1863 that would lead to a Yosemite park and facilitated the advent of the California Geological Survey (1863–1870) under state geologist Josiah Dwight Whitney. He also sought to abolish slavery and treat Chinese immigrants like human beings. When he proposed a Yosemite park, with land ceded to California, he made an interesting observation: That on the one hand Yosemite was for all public purpose worthless, but also contained some of the greatest wonders of the world. This idea was intriguing to President Abraham Lincoln.

I would still prefer that this mountain were named for some aspect of its place. Though there surely was one, I do not know the Native American name for this peak that rises above the influence of glaciers—so dominating the view, so purely granitic one could cry. Whorl Mountain too has its charms and is named, perhaps, for the botanical aspect of its three closely associated peaks. Matterhorn sits at the head of the canyon of Spiller Creek.

Whoever decided to name Yosemite's much less prominent and considerably more straightforwardly structured granite crag a Matterhorn didn't care about how it was made. This kind of naming reveals a great deal about American culture, but not about the rock itself. People have died on all of these mountains. Sometimes as the mountains change they take humans along, as Edward Whymper learned during the first ascent of the European Matterhorn, whose tectonic history is also interesting and elaborate.[5]

The ensemble of these summits marks the northern edge of a region of granite wedges, serrated edges, and huge blocks. Yet Conness dominates like a huge tombstone. How exactly is one to feel, when it sometimes seems like being in a cemetery surrounded by monuments? How do the dead feel about their headstones? How do those still alive interpret these mountains as signs made of rock? However I feel about this mountain called Conness, I have ascended this granite many times by multiple routes, with Valerie and others, with many I loved, including my son.

The summit of Conness is by no means a pristine wilderness. Because of its centrality, it was a natural site for surveying the region. From the 1870s and periodically through the twentieth century, elaborate structures and concrete piers were constructed on the summit and south shoulder of the peak by the USGS to allow surveyors to live and work while measuring surrounding altitudes.[6] Nor is the ascent from the shoulder to the summit virgin rock. After one passes the detritus of posts and pillars, some fenced, a hiker following the easiest route ascends a staircase built from its shoulder to the summit.

Agile and silent as he steps across the broken rock near the peak, a slim boy in his mid-teens, half a foot taller than me, shirtless this August afternoon, tan, his dark hair riffling in the breeze, with his wry look of dark humor—a shade of melancholy in his eyes mirroring my own, indeterminate. I remember my son on this summit. I never worried about Jesse when he was in the mountains.

We turn away. Once again we begin our almost ritualistic itinerary, mostly following the same program every year, visiting the same summits, wandering in various directions in no particular order until, after a while, we get our bearings, remember the feel of the rock under foot and return. This granite is a place to which one must return, for there is no lasting or final reconciliation with rock, only a temporary accommodation to its discipline. So we return each year, expecting nothing and not disappointed. The rock has nothing to say; yet we listen.

Granite at Sunrise

Granite as hieroglyph.

WE KNOW THE Sierra batholith emerged sometime after the Farallon Plate subducted below the North American Plate, approximately 150 to 80 million years ago.[1] But "why is granite granite?"—as a friend once told me his geology professor asked, posing a nearly theological question, especially when one contemplates the Tuolumne Intrusive Suite. Herman Melville entertains the same question when he writes of the "wrinkled granite hieroglyphics" of the Rosetta stone, itself composed of black granodiorite though because of its color for many years thought to be basalt.

At a distance, any granite can appear dark or light. Especially when up high, in early morning light, perhaps on the granodiorite slabs north of Mount Hoffman.[2] At the edge of the suite, I turn and behold an assemblage of dark forms: Half Dome, Quarter Domes, Tenaya Peak, Fairview, Lembert Dome, Dog Dome, Ragged Peak, the Matthes Crest, Mount Conness, Cathedral Peak, Dana, Gibbs, on and on. This view encompasses a great deal of what I care about. Granite at dawn viewed from the west, its features hidden in shadow. Later on this day, granite in the light, glistening folds, creases, wrinkles.

I have allowed the Tuolumne Intrusive Suite to become exactly a wrinkled hieroglyphic of myself, "a key to some previously undecipherable mystery or unattainable understanding," crucial to decrypting some essential code, a microcosm whose secrets reveal some truth of a larger whole. No uniform hiero-glyphic or sacred carving exists for granite—or else it is all sa-cred. Because granite is ubiquitous: It is the stuff of continental stability, everywhere underfoot but rarely visible. Here in the Sierra Nevada, where it shows its face, "I put that brow before you. Read it if you can," I say to myself, as if I were asked the question Melville posed.[3]

If only granite were animate, I could say about it, "Granite sees the light: Absorbs and reflects it. The same granite, heated by sun and cooled by frost, has seen great ice and has born up under a burden of blue light." I walk on granite now, cold, warm, and sometimes hot—distant, alien, welcoming, and frightening. I watch my step. There are many ways to know granite, up close and from afar. There are many ways to get up close, by circumnavigation, ascent, traverse, descent. At one time, ascent was everything to me. Now I circumnavigate. I have become less ambitious and more circumspect.

Granite is never featureless, always grained—"phaneritic," a geology teacher says: It has visible crystals. When it decom-poses, these crystals become scree, a seemingly uniform sea of gems. Scree is not sand, but something coarser and brighter. Granite has myriad surfaces, rough and smooth. Though these surfaces change under aspects of light, yet granite has no face.

The granite humans experience is a tiny portion of the gran-ite of the world, uncounted grains hidden from sight or touch, the basement of our continents. Granite seems to sleep under our feet. It awakens in the mountains in many forms available to touch. No need to search for it because it reaches toward the sky. Some forms remain just out of reach—these horns and pinnacles on high, some intimidating. Angular blocks and dark dihedrals weather in shadows and sun; great slabs adorn domes where one breathes easily. In Tenaya Canyon smooth massive walls reflect riffling waters. Sometimes too steep, sometimes almost flat, granite sometimes becomes an entry to other worlds.

This rock has its own evolutionary history though it cannot be said to adapt. What once was shaped by heat and immense pressure now has been shaped by more temperate elements: wind, ice, lightning, and sun. This range of light—whose heart is rock—might be named for the granite's light now that it is no longer the Sierra Nevada.

Indeed, one begins to wonder what Muir meant by "Range of Light." According to one interpretation, Muir saw "a wonderland of durable, light-colored granite": "It is this geology that makes the Sierra a 'Range of Light' shining brightly across the Central Valley even late in summer."[4] This was not all what Muir meant when he iterated a panoply of kinds of light offered by the Sierra:

> And after ten years spent in the heart of it, rejoicing and wondering, bathing in its glorious floods of light, seeing the sunbursts of morning among the icy peaks, the noonday radiance on the trees and rocks and snow, the flush of the alpenglow, and a thousand dashing waterfalls with their marvelous abundance of irised spray, it still seems to me above all others the Range of Light, the most divinely beautiful of all the mountain-chains I have ever seen.[5]

But we may be getting there—to a world of rock without ice, trees, or water.

Granite exfoliates: Granite endures. The walks I take leave few footprints. I hurry to inhabit these glacial surfaces as if they might decompose soon. Their contours make sense, their flows shadow ghosts of glacial flow, their hidden origins. Granite takes and holds shapes of forces beyond me—and perfects them: I stand within the past and look around, imagining ice while touching rock.

One can speak of the petrology, the chemical and crystalline structure of these igneous rocks, and distinguish granite from granodiorite, or quartz monzonite, but not the speciation of it. Granite is everywhere but is nowhere the same. Granite is not homogeneous. One can speak of the meaning of granite, or even the why of it, but what counts for me is to experience it.

This leads back to diurnal matters. Every day the rocks reappear: Their forms return to clarity, surfaces shine. Almost every day, granite warms in the sun and remains cool in the shadows. Warm granite is good for after a swim. Cool granite is good for shade on a hot day. We abide with granite gladly. Contact.

Yet granite can be exacting. Granite in full summer sun becomes an oven. Granite in the autumn shade numbs fingers and chills the soul. What expands or contracts is not only the rock, but also the mind. Granite absorbs and releases energy in its diurnal cycle. In other words, it has thermal properties, absorbing and conducting heat. Thermodynamics speaks of specific heat capacity and conductivity. The specific heat capacity of granite is 790 calories per gram degree Celsius. Not so very high, but compared to what?

Granite and other rocks high in silicate minerals have a lower percentage of the heavier elements and are correspondingly enriched in the lighter elements—silicon, oxygen, aluminum, and potassium. These are called *felsic*. This made-up word fuses FEL for feldspar and SIC for silica. Of these light-colored minerals some geologists speak poetically, saying that granite "represents the purified end product of the Earth's internal differentiation process."[6]

Granite is coming into being even as I speak of its seasons and senses. This rock I traverse is well-seasoned, for millions of years. Like all things, granite experiences metamorphosis. Structures appear within its matrix long before they appear on the surface of the Earth.

Though it is good to keep one's feet on rock, to make connections, these connections change. Sometimes, late in fall, our feet touch smooth stained granite where water used to run and will again. The granite that we experience in winter is sometimes covered with ice, with water running underneath. In the spring, rocky rifts dance with white water, sounds of water shaped by forms of their courses. In summer it warms.

The experience of granite is not well represented by the crafts of photography. What one sees is only what one sees: close-ups, foregrounds, middle grounds, and backgrounds. Geologists are notoriously though not universally poor photographers, especially when composing their images by placing a pencil, hammer, coin, or other object in the midst to give the photo "scale." What a landscape is—is another question. Yes, granite is wider than it is high. Yes, many of its forms have aesthetic appeal. More specifically, and more intimately, granite appeals to educated and even indoctrinated senses and may in fact ground them.

One such sense is memory. So I speak of remembering granite, reminding myself of the rock. Having spent a long time in intimate relations, I can assert that granite is visible in few places: it is hidden in most others. But on any day, one can touch granite, feel it with hands, feet, any part of the body. It is a reliable resource. One can smell granite, perhaps taste it. One can hear granite or hear the spaces that granite makes. Yet by its presence, granite reveals the void.

You might say my obsession with granite reveals my privilege to spend a great deal of time here, much of that time within a national park. Privilege also has its costs because granite is a hard mother. It will not return a touch. This suits my sense of reality in more than one way. Because I fool myself with sentiment about this rock, it is best to find granite intimidating, especially when considering a climb of a large rock. One ought to be properly respectful. And yet I admit I am fond of granite, to excess. This rock does not waste my time.

I read, for instance, about "15 breathtaking views of the world that will make you dizzy with wonder."[7] I am not a seeker of breathtaking views. Nor do I desire a "luxury home with breathtaking views," or wish to pursue stunning views from space. Sublime views are all well and fine. Even scientists speak of "breathtaking views of the cerebellar neuronal circuitry." Long views, short views: People count them, collect them, climb them, photograph them—as a certain kind of performance.[8] My performance is somewhat different, perhaps introspective, but not necessarily better. This is granite, I say, unlike anything else I confront. It requires nothing of me. I don't have to mourn for it. I don't have to fear for it. Yet I can touch it with all my senses, as if it were real and eternal.

This is Not a Mountain

Can the language of granitic rocks be simplified?

ACCORDING TO CERTAIN practices of science, "all things on Earth can be seen as at once objects and archives." Which is to say, "a rock can be read as an object that constitutes part of the lithosphere and equally as a document that contains its own history written into it."[1] Geoffrey C. Bowker refers to this dual perspective as the basis for what he calls "memory practices of the sciences" that commit certain observations to record, as in scientific papers. Scientists, and all of us, record memories "within a range of practices (technical, formal, social) that . . . [allow] . . . useful/interesting descriptions of the past to be carried forward into the future." The notion of an open past, Bowker concludes, has the potential to "unlock the present and free the future."[2]

My memory practices are somewhat different because they read Tuolumne's rocks as objects that not only contain their own history, but also reveal my own history—and I suspect that secretly this is also true for geologists. When I narrate certain walks, I map geology too.

Political maps and topographical maps hide the true matter underfoot, typically being rectangular and arbitrary in their boundaries. Granite does not follow the political boundaries of nations, states, wilderness areas, or national parks. We cannot take them for *granite*. Also, there is no *geo-logic* of political maps. Granite is all contingent, three-dimensional and dynamic. The maps I own are flat projections and mnemonic devices.

I study the "Geologic Map of the Mono Craters Quadrangle" that includes a depiction of the place in June Lake, California, where we live seasonally. The "granite" domes behind our cabin are labeled Wheeler Crest Quartz Monzonite. (Mind you, these juniper-strewn domes didn't come from the Wheeler Crest; the mineral was only identified there.) Up toward the left-hand top corner of the quad is the Dana Plateau: The Third Pillar, made of the Quartz Monzonite of Ellery Lake or perhaps of Lee Vining Canyon, is unnoted (not posted), though it is a stunning landmark for anyone who enters Lee Vining Canyon, and an exceptional climb. I memorize these geological names. You can see from this same geologic map that things get complicated around Tioga Pass. I cannot keep the names of all these kinds of rocks straight. A lot of prose has been written about these complexities.

People like me—rock climbers, ex-rock climbers—choose the simplest rock we can because it is safer and more predictable. So we also choose a simpler terminology. But we know that any seemingly simple rock is embedded in a more complicated pattern—as we can see from maps and photos.[3]

What's worse, most of what we call granite is probably classified as something slightly and subtly different. Because some climbers are interested in geology, this leads to discussions about the actual name for the rock underfoot. But does it really matter for our experience? Most climbers continue to speak of Yosemite's rock as granite, though much of it is more properly "granitic rock" or a "granitoid." "After all," as a contributor to the climber's forum at Supertopo named Minerals writes, "there is more granodiorite in the Sierra Nevada Batholith than there is granite. And there is diorite too, right? So, what's the difference?" He then provides a lucid précis of

Yosemite mineralogy which is illustrated by a well-known triangular QAP (quartz-alkali feldspars-plagioclase feldspars)
diagram found in many petrology textbooks: a mountain-
like abstraction of related granitic rocks where Q = quartz,
A = alkali/potassium feldspar, and P = plagioclase feldspar
(see figure 25.1). I study this diagram, thinking of granite as
a palimpsest, granite as consistent with certain principles of
ordering, as if it could be enclosed in a classification system.
"To classify is Human," as Geoffrey C. Bowker and Susan
Leigh Star explain in *Sorting Things Out: Classification and
its Consequences.*[4] As I understand the problems entailed,
not only is it difficult to define classification as a "a spatial,
temporal, or spatio-temporal segmentation of the world," but
as I learned in rhetorical analysis, successful classification

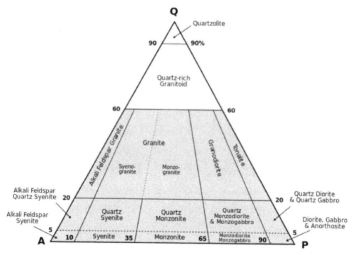

FIGURE 25.1. QAP Figure: Triangular Plutonic Rock Classification
Source: Figure based on R. W. Le Maitre et al., (editor), *Igneous
Rocks: A Classification and Glossary of Terms, Recommendations
of the International Union of Geological Sciences Subcommission
on the Systematics of Igneous Rocks*, 2nd edition. (Cambridge, UK:
Cambridge University Press, 2002)

depends on consistency of principles, mutually exclusive categories, completeness. Hence the QAP chart:

    The person called Minerals considers three pieces of rock:

1. One with "50% quartz and 50% feldspar . . . potassium feldspar making up 65% of the total feldspar in the rock and plagioclase feldspar making up 35%": This would be granite.
2. One with "30% quartz and 70% feldspar, with potassium
   feldspar making up 20% of the total feldspar and plagioclase
   feldspar making up 80%": This would be granodiorite.
3. One with "10% quartz and 90% feldspar, with potassium
   feldspar making up 5% of the total feldspar and plagioclase
   feldspar making up 95%": This would be quartz diorite.[5]

This can go on and on. The mind spins.[6] Yet it is surely true
that normal hikers and climbers will notice subtle differences
in color and shape and texture of rock, in how it does or
doesn't fragment, without being able to precisely identify one
granitic type from another or engage in the tongue-twisters
required to name them or sort them out.

    Quartz monzonite sits right above the center of the base of
this pyramidal diagram. Just so, in Lee Vining Canyon, quartz
monzonite of Ellery Lake, Wheeler Crest quartz monzonite,
granodiorite of Mono Dome, and quartz monzonite of Lee
Vining Canyon sit near each other. These names come from
Kistler's 1966 Mono Craters geological quadrangle, which uses
a somewhat superseded granitic classification scheme.[7] It is
hard to know what I have learned by studying classification by
diagram and map.

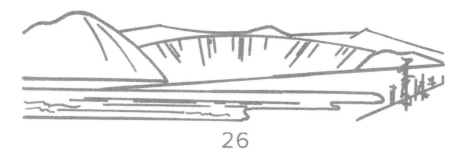

Granite as Enigma

Things we don't know about granite and ourselves.

The study of history of any kind depends upon documents and records. For the history of the Earth's crust, these documents are the rocks and their reading and interpretation are often difficult operations.

H.H. READ, *The Granite Controversy* (1957)[1]

NO MATTER HOW CAREFULLY classified, rocks remain somewhat obscure documents and geologists argue about interpretations of them. "Granites are among the most enigmatic rocks of the Earth's continental crust." So writes the geologist Antonio Castro. He wonders redundantly "why these apparently simple rocks, mostly composed of quartz and feldspars, are so enigmatic."[2]

For their own reasons, geologists have a propensity to speak of enigmas. An enigma, according to the dictionary, "conceals a hidden meaning or known thing under obscure words or forms" so that an enigma might be a "dark saying, or riddle," and this riddle becomes a tale, a story, perhaps a saying or proverb whose sense is "inexplicable to an observer." What enigma can be imagined here, under one's feet? Who can one ask?

In this matter, granite shows restraint, does not boast, remains silent about its origins and intentions. Granite refuses to talk of its own history. Nothing is more obscure than granite. Granite just is. In such silences, neither ancient nor modern, where solid rock refrains from speech, the human mind is caught in an enigma.

Granite here is concrete and yet enigmatic, especially to geologists, because no one can fully understand its origins, having little ability to reach down below the crust of the Earth for empirical data. Where is it made, how is it made, and of what original constituents? a geologist might ask. But many might agree with Edward Abbey, who is "pleased enough with the surfaces—in fact they alone seem to me to be of much importance . . . the bark of a tree, the abrasion of granite and sand, the plunge of clear water into a pool, the face of the wind— what else is there? What else do we need?"[3]

For others, surfaces are not enough. Why else would anyone constantly ask questions of geologists, or why would anyone be reading all these professional articles? Why be interested in the history of the earth when one can simply walk upon, can touch the solid rock that contains its own history?

Though humans cannot get inside rocks, they can get between them. Children, for instance, love to sneak between the surfaces in gullies, chimneys, slits, and windows, often tearing their clothes to shreds. Yet rocks are essentially obscure. The inside of a rock calls for remote sensing.

So too with the inside of human consciousness. What do we know about what is inside another? Whatever it means to know a person is not what it means to know rock. (What *does* it mean to know a person?) The obdurate nature of rock is and is not like the obdurate nature of human minds. Because rock does not speak, rock neither lies nor tells the truth. Rock has no rhetoric. Rock reminds humans of the limits to knowledge.

As a human gets older, the mind may—as we say—petrify, but the words keep flowing. Under such circumstances, is it better to desire commerce with inanimate objects that do not waste words? They will not die. But what ecstasy lives in rocks?

You can look at a granite monolith and make it into scenery or more. Valerie and I spend much of our time in June Lake, California. Our local scenic mountain, Carson Peak, named for the first proprietor of Silver Lake Resort, appears regularly as the background in advertisements for sport utility vehicles. Made of quartz monzonite of Lee Vining Canyon, according to my map, it also appears in advertisements for tourists as the "Swiss Alps of the Sierra." But, as I have said repeatedly, if you want to realize rock, you have to touch it, transform a two-dimensional scene into something with depth. Smell it! Consider the smell of Carson Peak's cold-shaded cliffs, sun-warmed ledges, or wet slabs. Touch it. Lick it. The tongue knows.

It is a hard world where granite predominates on the surface: very little soil, very little vegetation in the river, scrawny fish humans planted here. Granite is not generous to life. Granite is hard. Especially cold, in the shadows, early, just after dawn—put your hand upon it! You can feel that hardness and coldness are sisters: Granite is unforgiving. There seems nothing comic, nothing contingent about granite. It endures.

What of this hardness, one wonders. Compared only to other minerals? No, compared to other things one might encounter regularly. Granite is harder than sandstone but softer than quartz, harder than obsidian. It is sometimes the hardest rock to climb upon, yet often the simplest. Things are quite straightforward, if difficult.

Yet granite is light. Granite floats, or so we are told, above the magma. Granite bursts into the air and rises, forming the backbones of mountain ranges. The granite that I admire here in the Sierra, studded with feldspar, may be made of melted sediments. So it might be true that "the rocks of this planet are almost entirely modified by life," as Gaia Vince argues in *Adventures in the Anthropocene*.[4]

Granite, in a sense, is both labile and outstanding. Climbers

go to granite because it reaches toward the sky—and imagine
this as aspiration, as an emblem of something in themselves
that rises. We know it is not true, and yet we sing along to
Jefferson Airplane's "Crown of Creation," "Life is change: How
it's different from the rocks."

We loved to climb upon it because we believed we had
honed our skills and wouldn't be killed unless it was our fault.
Our sense of granite was straightforward because hard rock
rarely provides what climbers call objective danger. Subjective
danger was another matter. Sleeping on granite has never been
easy—and try to pitch a tent! This hardness, this sleeplessness,
permits one to trust and to fear.

The distant grayness of rock suggests sameness, but nothing could be further from the truth; this is not grayness but a
speckle of minerals—hornblende, biotite, quartz, feldspar—in
various proportions. Rock is scarcely ever homogeneous.

Only ten of the perhaps seven thousand known minerals
make up more than 95% of Earth's crust and almost all are
silicate minerals. "Most abundant silicates are feldspars (plagioclase (39%) and alkali feldspar (12%)). Other common silicate minerals are quartz (12%), pyroxenes (11%), amphiboles
(5%), micas (5%), and clay minerals (5%). The rest of the silicate family comprises 3% of the crust. Only 8% of the crust is
composed of non-silicates—carbonates, oxides, sulfides, etc."[5]

I choose from those silicates to know feldspars first. I know
feldspar with my hand as it weathers, and know it by its shape
within the mosaics of texture that grace these glacially polished
domes. Feldspar: the hard rock that does not contain ore, or a
hard rock that cleaves cleanly—so guesses at etymology suggest.

Granite is not simple stuff, and yet it seems to have made
me simpleminded. Maybe it was wrong to spend my time
climbing upon granite landmarks, wrong to imagine any three
dimensions to my time here. On the other hand, as Thoreau

intones, "Our life is frittered away by detail. Simplify, simplify."
So I did—and abstracted too.

What is left to risk, now that my climbing days are done? I
have been assured by those who know better that I continue to
engage in the usual thought-errors to which environmentalists
are prone, that my sense of granite as eternal and everlasting is
illusory. The ecocritic and author Jeremy Davies speaks of this
as the *David Brower syndrome*, "making it sound as if change
in the Earth system is abnormal, thereby collapsing the history
of the planet into a single dichotomy between ancient natural
stillness and modern anthropogenic depravity."[6]

Though others may, I cannot live within the largest scales
of time. I fail to comprehend geological time in any personal
way. I imagine that a rock I recognize will remain beyond my
life and be, in that sense, eternal. No doubt I am wrong.

For several summers, when Valerie and I lived in a log cabin
in Tuolumne Meadows overlooking Soda Springs, we used an
outhouse that had an exquisite view of Unicorn Peak out the
open door, the same view that Ansel Adams famously photo-
graphed—though not from our outhouse. As we took turns there
every morning, the peak gleamed, and throughout summer we
watched as snow receded from its flanks. I visited that summit
many times, climbed all over it from many directions, once with
my six-year-old son on a day of vigorous thunderstorm weather,
clouds pouring in from the southwest. We descended from the
summit, racing to get down before lightning found us, me holding his hand. I told him, "Be careful here, the snow can be rotten
next to the rock," right before I dropped through the crust, still
holding his hand, looking up at his surprise. We left that peak in
rain and hail and the constant cracks of thunder, he untroubled
in his silly blue rain suit and me in my dark thoughts.

An Edge of History:
An Edge of a Continent

The Dana Plateau.

A COUPLE THOUSAND FEET above Tioga Pass (at 9,943 feet or 3,031 meters), just outside of Yosemite National Park, one looks up toward the Dana Plateau (at 12,466 feet or 3,800 meters). This place, we are told, is one of those "anomalous areas with gently rolling surfaces that escaped glacial sculpting." The Dana Plateau did not escape the elements, nor does anyone who goes there. Known by climbers as the approach to and top of the notable climb on the Third Pillar, it is composed of a medium-grained mineral known as quartz monzonite of Ellery Lake, which is maybe 98 million years old. This plateau constitutes an edge between the Sierra Nevada and the Great Basin—but for me it is an edge between other things as well.

It is also a surface, so that one can imagine this area—according to N. King Huber, one of the elegant geological writers on Yosemite—as an "unglaciated remnant of an ancient land surface sharply truncated by glacial cirques."[1]

Going to the Dana Plateau is a little like entering a dream—up through that field of partially buried rounded boulders, high in the sky. A herd of boulders you might say, and according to the geologists these "frost-heaved joint blocks" were subject to cycles of cold and heat that broke the bedrock along fractures, heaved the remnants, and smoothed and rounded each one by wind-driven sand.

At the crest, at the top of the continent, many of these boulders possess little potholes, sometimes containing rainwater as they did the last time I came here. Animals drink here. I have been to this place with three different dogs, the first named by my son for the mountain whose north face shadows to the south.

It is hard to see these boulders as the geologists do, as jumbled blocks. No, when one approaches this high field of white and gray boulders, a sense of comfort and even peace comes, despite the wind, and one enters an ancient granite garden. Each boulder seems a little monument; each has a symmetry of its own and a significance. Or else each seems like a tilted gravestone.

As the geologist N. King Huber would prefer to say: "These upland surfaces have a significance far beyond being unglaciated, because they are very ancient." His antiquarian sentiment is engaged because "they are remnants of the gently rolling terrain that existed here before the late Cenozoic uplift," they stand above the "incision of the Sierra that began about 25 million years ago." The Cenozoic: an era of new life, of mammals, and eventually of us. These "upland areas near the stream headwaters were the last to be affected: some remnants still remain undissected."[2]

Undissected. One is on the edge of something here. On the one hand, there is a calm that comes from wandering through old places, perhaps because of the perspective one gains. Old places endure. From the repose of this granite garden, one views the even older rocks of Mount Dana proper. One is glad to be in a place that lacks sharp edges. At this place on the top of a continent, the Dana Plateau is also the edge of a precipice. Climbing the higher pitches of the Third Pillar, one is happy to discover that these sharp edges provide better hand and footholds as the pitches steepen.

Strangely enough, this undissected plateau is geologically similar to the edge of the helmeted summit of Mount Whitney, where wasting blocks of aplite are stacked.[3]

What then is a continent and how does one know where the edge might be? A continent is from the Latin *terra continens,* "continuous land," but also self-restraining, holding together. This North American continent has many edges, some far inland from the ocean. Wherever granite is underfoot, there one stands on the edge of a continent, or so I would like to think. But according to another view, "Despite being more than one hundred miles inland from the geographic edge of the continent, the Sierra Nevada is, geodetically speaking, not really a part of North America."[4]

Of what then is it a part? As I remember, Carl Sharsmith used to take students here. After climbing nearly to the Sierra's crest, they would have to lie on their stomachs to visit what he referred to as "belly plants." This is the posture of one who studies low-lying alpine botany. Because the Dana Plateau is a *nunatak,* an island that remained above ancient glacial paths, it hosts a diverse selection of pre-ice age or relict biota. Supposedly half the alpine plants found in the Sierra can be found there.

In multiple senses, the Dana Plateau has been imagined to be an island. So, too, in *An Island Called California* (1971), Elna Bakker called upon a claim in a sixteenth-century novel by Garci Rodríguez de Montalvo "that on the right hand of the Indies there is an island called California very close to the side of the Terrestrial Paradise." She speaks of this narrative as a tangle of fact and fiction. Bakker's purpose is to argue that the biota of California constitute an island.[5]

However, geology is no longer as it seemed for her in 1971. Plate tectonics arrived and continued to complicate itself. For instance, "the widely accepted explanation posits that the oceanic Farallon plate acted as a conveyor belt, sweeping terranes into the continental margin while subducting under it . . . which fails to explain many terrane complexities, is also inconsistent with new tomographic images of lower-mantle slabs, and with their locations relative to plate reconstructions."[6]

Now, researchers at UCLA and elsewhere use a technique called seismic tomography to study the deep structure of the Pacific plate, one of nearly a dozen major plates at the surface of the earth: They measure and image thickness, the interior of the plate, and the underlying mantle; they can estimate the direction of flow of rocks in the mantle.

Geophysicist Caroline Beghein explains, "Rocks deform and flow slowly inside the Earth's mantle, which makes the plates move at the surface. . . . Our research enables us to image the interior of the plate and helps us figure out how it formed and evolved." Yet Beghein admits that fundamental properties of plates "are still somewhat enigmatic."[7]

As a result of these techniques of imaging, geophysicists have mapped the very roots of the Sierra and found it "geodetically speaking, not really part of North America."[8] In which case we can imagine the Dana Plateau as an island nested in the Sierra Nevada, itself an island embedded someplace near the edge of a continent.

On these highest surfaces, alpine plants inhabit many so-called "alpine fellfields" like those on the Dana Plateau—stony habitats with meager shallow soils, high in the sky, sparsely inhabited, and important.[9] These plants are almost always perennials, and since some characteristically develop as a mat or cushion, are called "cushion plants." Their low stature and compact forms are adapted to the alpine habitat; they are efficient heat traps that decouple their temperature from the surrounding air, generating thermal differences between leaves and the air as high as 20°C. Not only that, but they contain a disproportionately greater abundance of other plant species inside their cushions than outside. Cushions are good nurse plants because they provide thermal refuges and water storage. They are not so much relict as foundational because they constitute *refugia*, refuges where the future biota of the Sierra is rooted, havens for alpine ecosystems.[10]

I continue to the east edge of the Dana Plateau, to the top of the Third Pillar, and peer down at geological history, down Lee Vining Creek toward Mono Lake's closed drainage basin at 6,378.1 feet (1,946 meters). Turning toward the west, I might contemplate the mysteries of exfoliation gracing the headwaters of the Tuolumne River, whereby glaciated granitic surfaces, monoliths and little hills retain their shapes while sloughing off their surfaces. Here in this autumn of rock, when domes of granite below strip off their surfaces, flakes fall as if they were sloughing off some live body. Those domes one can liken to plants stripped of leaves.

Why expect rock to renew itself—or offer a second face to the world, so similar to the first? How can such a process be managed? Why speak of this process as "weathering," or as if rock had skin? Joints and sheets, someone says. We speak of whole sheets peeling instead of grains coming apart.

Granite is by definition granular, but that is not how its heart behaves—as if some tension resides within. Yet the leaves or slabs that come off weather themselves by losing grains and become grains; boulders become pocked and pocketed, as if breathing in knots and clicks. I imagine those grains going to the sea.

Humans mystify granite in the way they talk about it, using their strange languages of surfaces. Humans think of writing on surfaces. Humans are speaking to surfaces. *Ex Folio*, for instance, from the book: surfaces containing words. Historians imagine people writing upon the leaves of trees. A folio might be a single sheet of paper folded once and on this paper a hieroglyphic. And then words on rocks. A hieroglyph itself has its origin as a sacred carving, sculpted mark, or symbol. Of what? The peak to the south, named in 1863 by the Whitney Survey for James Dwight Dana (1813–1895), who studied mountain building, volcanism, and the origin of continents and was best known for his books on mineralogy. We name mountains for each other. We write our names in summit registers.

Beyond management by us, the rock renews its surfaces. All else is only words.

Although touching granite is satisfactory enough, it is good to know the history of those things one loves to touch. Because granite has been formed on or near the edges of continents, one walks on granite near the edge of things as we land-dwelling animals know them. Also, having spent a great deal of time sitting on granite, I have noticed a certain coldness. I revere that coldness.

This coldness, this fear at the edge of things, what is it? What is an edge, and how do I know when I approach one? Edges take many forms and sometimes can be found far inland, but always indicate changes in the surface of the earth. This seems to contradict the intuitive sense of solidity and permanence of granite cliffs. An edge between sea and land, between life and death, between one world and another. An edge between myself and this granite upon which I sit or walk.

John Muir glorified the edge of the mountains from his perspective at Mono Lake, where he saw "the mighty barren Sierra rising abruptly from the water to a height of seven thousand feet, and stretching north and south for twenty miles with rows of snowy peaks. Ranges of cumulus clouds swelling in massive bosses of pearl—cloud mountains and rock mountains equally grand and substantial in appearance."[11]

Mono Lake is one place where the Sierra marks the edge of the Great Basin to the east—or vice versa. But something is missing here. Whatever the Sierra might be, in Muir's passage it is so far distant that it is unreal. This walker wants to touch the edge, wants real matter—as a friend once referred to it, reminding his readers of his source in yet another writer who paraphrases a third.[12]

"The closer you get to real matter, rock air fire wood, boy, the more spiritual the world is," writes Kerouac in *The Dharma Bums*, paraphrasing Gary Snyder.[13] This granite, this ground, might be both substantial and a state of affairs, might be a particular substance that occupies space or a daunting situation. Matter comes down to us through texts. This matter of granite, then, might be both internal and external: the rock, the granite batholith, yet also some methods of confronting it closely. Paul Wienpahl (1916–1980), a philosopher who hailed from Rock Springs, Wyoming, but made his life at UC Santa Barbara, wrote my favorite book on meditation: *The Matter of Zen*. As he puts it, "A mystery is made of a matter, the matter, which is mysterious only in its simplicity."[14] There are no mysteries as matters of fact, or so we are told. A life consists of encounters that matter. I sit here to continue my one-sided appointment with granite.

According to the famous rock climber Royal Robbins, "When I touched the rock, it had in turn touched my spirit . . . awakening an ineffable longing, as if I had stirred a hidden memory of a previous existence, a happier one. While I was climbing, it was glorious to be alive."[15]

I am attracted to granite and intimidated—especially by its textures—precisely because it is not flesh. It doesn't feel like flesh; it does not return my touch. It is without senses, without responses. Though it cannot touch my spirit, my spirit may choose to touch it. Granite requires nothing of me. Granite is silent, steadfast, everlasting. Granite is without brother or sister, kinship, relationship, love, friendship, or happiness, yet provides a kind of peace because it is not of me, or with me. Granite does not care and does not expect care. It resides at the edge of everything and nothing.

Epilogue: Ventifacts

Petromorphism, here and now.

"And see, it is not so sad a place as one might think.
Look, there is the sky, and here is the grass."
"I know where I am," he replied,
but would say nothing more, and so I left him.

HERMAN MELVILLE, "Bartleby the Scrivener"[1]

From what I've tasted of desire
I hold with those who favor fire.

ROBERT FROST "Fire and Ice"

ACCORDING TO NASA, "about half of the rocks at the Mars Pathfinder Ares Vallis landing site appear to be ventifacts, rocks abraded by windborne particles . . . including rocks with faceted edges, finger-like projections, elongated pits, flutes, grooves, and possible rills."[2] Aeolian geology studies these elaborate and multifaceted objects.

This discipline called "Aeolian Research" reminds a literary scholar of the Aeolian harp (or lyre), the wind harp named for Aeolus, Greek god in charge of the winds. The German Jesuit Athanasius Kircher designed a wooden box containing eight to twelve strings stretched over two bridges and tuned in unison, placed where the wind draws out a harmonious sound. This idea and its embodiment emerges as an irresistible symbol in a poem by Samuel Taylor Coleridge: "And what if all of animated nature / Be but organic Harps diversely fram'd, / That tremble into thought, as o'er them sweeps / Plastic and vast, one intellectual breeze, / At once the Soul of each, and God of all?"[3]

One can also find granite ventifacts in Antarctic dry valleys. One can find them in Joshua Tree National Park. These are artifacts upon which the wind has played. What are called ventifacts or windkanters are not commonly found in Yosemite though one occasionally runs across similar wind-formed shapes, especially on summits.

These artifacts of the wind—abraded, etched, grooved, sculpted, and smoothed by wind-driven sand or ice crystals— why seek them on the level when on almost any exposed high granite ridge almost anywhere in this region one can handle similar wind-blown surfaces, so that every summit seems like a unique artifact?

Being coarse-grained, granite is not always turned glass-like by wind-driven particles, though most often made smooth by water-driven particles under glaciers and in riverbeds. People are fascinated by these wind shapes because they are rare, and because they seem graceful. A particular type of ventifact is the *dreikanter*, the German name indicating three surfaces: A kind of miniature pyramid whose facets have been shaped by blowing sand. You can place one on your desk.

In the same vein, some people collect "suiseki," or scholar's stones. "Suiseki devotees (Sui = water, Seki = stone) study and enjoy naturally formed stones as objects of beauty." For multiple reasons, these stones of pleasing shapes and textures suggest mountains, lakes, waterfalls, and other natural scenes. As one aficionado says, "They represent nature in the palm of your hand."[4] Such "viewing stones," have their own elaborate cultural history. Granite is a preferred medium for them.

Or else, "*Suiseki* [水石], is an abbreviation of the term *sansui keiseki*, which approximately translates as landscape view or scenery stone. These might be a cornerstone of traditional Japanese aesthetics, adopted from China through Korea. Chinese enthusiasts think of 'imaginative stones' as '*gongshi*' or '*guai shi*' ('fantastic' or 'strange stones'). In Korea, some are known as '*useok*' ('eternal stones')."[5]

In the palm of your hand; on the top of your desk! Can anyone hold these granitic domes of Tuolumne Meadows in the palm of a hand? I hear a familiar voice: "Where wast thou when I laid the foundations of the Earth? declare, if thou hast understanding." There they are, in the moonlight. Here I am. Here is my hand. There is something else still glued to this form in the night. When I was young, I carved a representation of El Capitan from pine: It had the aspect of a sleeping or kneeling giant.

The granite of Yosemite in moonlight arrests our attention. Insomnia comes when the results of wind or water on rock alter consciousness. Why have we lived so long—so as to appreciate these rocks that are older than human monuments?

There is nothing wild about rock, but nothing tame or domestic either. You might say that contemplating an emptiness is only of value when one has nothing better to do, or as a kind of punishment or penance. You could call this lifelong contemplation a kind of narcissism. One anthology about rock climbing is entitled *Mirrors in the Cliffs*.[6] For someone like me—as climber or scholar—who cares to look? Why would they?

I might have devoted my entire life to climbing. Instead, I went to school, largely because I did not wish to go to war in the mid-1960s. When the war in Vietnam forced my return from Yosemite to graduate school, I sought an escape into literary studies, joining Valerie in this enterprise and eventually finding refuge in reading and writing. "History is a nightmare from which I am trying to awake," I read in *Ulysses*. Nobody can. So be it.

As a result of my profession in literary studies, Valerie and I have been situated inland, in or against western American mountains, for most of our adulthood. Over the years we have lived close to granite and close to sandstone. This has meant a great deal to us. We enjoyed being landlocked on the east side of the Sierra Nevada or the west side of the Colorado Plateau and have always thought of the Great Basin as a kind of mental space between them. When on the Colorado Plateau, we were Neptunists; when in the Sierra Nevada, Plutonists. Mostly we have been closer to granite and more plutonistic. Our region, like that of Switzerland or Afghanistan, is landlocked. We no longer crave the sea. This situation has allowed us to pay close attention to rock.

Granite is more flexible than one might imagine, especially if considering the way a human body can be engaged with it. Every rock climber knows about expanding flakes. But at large one must ask how minds are expanded when bodies engage with the elements—Earth, air, fire, water—and the many manifestations of those elements: rocks, rivers, lakes, trees, wildlife. But expanding flakes will someday fail.

As I have repeated over and over, we prefer rock that has been shaped by the elements, not by the hands of humans. For the present, nobody can make a Fairview Dome. Bodies of granite cannot be reproduced—not even by Ansel Adams, and certainly not by Walt Disney. Though these large forms are not works of art, it is impossible not to contemplate them aesthetically—but doing so secondhand seems somehow tawdry or, dare I say, meretricious. What authentic knowledge, using what senses?

Humans are increasingly implicated in geological processes, as powerful but crude agents. Humans are transitory. Geological processes, though not eternal, take a long time. In the long run, geological processes are exacting, as human processes never can be. Because we can configure rock in very minor and local ways—at least presently—that process is not what I am after here. I cannot guess about geoengineering in the future, or whether humans will someday create volcanoes. I am speaking about experiential senses. For instance: Can a person erupt in dance like a pluton, aspire like a spire? What did we mean when we used to speak of crack climbing, friction climbing, face climbing, if not that the body configures itself to the configurations of rock? I am more interested in the process of configuring ourselves to the world, rather than vice versa.

In my family, everyone learned early how to spread their arms like a sugar pine. These bodily gestures, cast as images of trees, are metaphors, like names. My middle name is Peter: like a rock. These gestures also express desires. Humans desire to change, to be more than themselves, to morph. But in which way, for what reasons, and to what end?

In mathematics, a morphism "refers to a structure-preserving map from one mathematical structure to another." When I spread my arms, I map the sugar pine. There are other kinds of more intuitive and various morphisms. We know that the suffix "morphic" is related to the name Morpheus, the god of dreams in Ovid, son of sleep, literally "the maker of shapes." The Greek suffix, *morphe*, names form, shape, figure, and in particular fine figure or beautiful form. We are told that Morpho was a nickname for Aphrodite.

To morph is to acquire or change shape. Consequently we can speak of phytomorphic activities, enacted by plants and also mimetically by insects, as a kind of shape shifting that is driven by forces inside and outside a living entity. Apparently people, too, like to imitate other living beings and to argue about the intelligence of animals, plants, or insects. And then there are holy plants, either considered to be divine or connected by imagery to gods.

I am primarily interested in conscious and deliberate human morphisms, anthropomorphic and petromorphic processes that humans choose. Maybe these are not entirely conscious acts, but they are conscious enough in retrospect, when they can be seen as choices that have been made.

I read in some arcane tract on philosophy that "an intrinsically existing thing is by definition petromorphic," permanent, self-marked, autonomous, self-sufficient. Consider my own very serious desire for petromorphism. "Aspiring to Rock Nature?" you ask. Imagine a mind in a petromorphic state.

Think of the heroic image of war in the *Iliad* where rocks resist waves, figuring "a petromorphic interpretation of human resistance," according to the philosopher Emmanuel Levinas (1906–1995).[7] I myself am more interested in the petromorphic interpretation of compliance, the mystical relation of hands and feet touching rock. Perhaps Levinas fears the effects of petromorphism for it implies the shunning of others. Though the rocklike form is somehow ultimately an unhuman form, humans have been seeing their own forms and faces in rocks forever. A petromorph is also a term describing the uneroded minerals of caves. Rock offers an invitation to turn toward the inhuman. It is not necessary to become unhuman just because one is attracted to rock. One does not need to become rock in order to approach rock closely and attentively. Rock is like wild things in this: It bears respect and safe distance.

There are rock-and-roll controversies about petromorphism: Paul Simon, "I am a rock. I am an island." Frank Zappa, "Help I'm a Rock!" Petromorphism, as a stance, is risky and dangerous in more than one way.

When alpine streams and rivers we love dwindle, they uncover golden stains on their beds. Glaciers melt and disappear, leaving polish and rubble in their wake. There will be less snow here in the future. Glaciologists speak of dead ice remaining when a glacier stalls and melts, leaving behind hummocky piles of glacio-fluvial sediment and kettle holes like those near Tioga Pass. Lakes recede, their hidden sources hiding year by year.

Pines lose some needles during drought and then turn brown. Massive fires come, darkening the sky. Creatures, large and small, lose their habitats, lose their ways and sometimes their lives. Small ones are poisoned by our chemicals. Species die out, as they always have. We make digital lists of these occurrences. And soon glaciologists in the arctic will be archaeologists.

Granite, sandstone, limestone endure in their many guises. You put your hands on rock, knowing you must trust them and knowing neither your hands nor the rock are permanent. When I climbed with Chuck Pratt, who we all considered a master, he tested every handhold. Granite is what we had to hang onto, and we did. Rock remains stronger and longer lasting than hands and feet, a last cold refuge, nobody's monument.

Notes

Introduction

1. Henry David Thoreau, *Walden*, vol. 1 (Boston: Houghton Mifflin, 1882), 8.
2. J. Baird Callicott and Michael P. Nelson, eds., *The Great New Wilderness Debate* (Athens: University of Georgia Press, 1998). Michael P. Nelson and J. Baird Callicott, eds., *The Wilderness Debate Rages On: Continuing the Great New Wilderness Debate* (Athens: University of Georgia Press, 2008). Roderick Nash, *Wilderness and the American Mind* (New Haven: Yale University Press, 1968).
3. The Wilderness Act, Public Law No. 88-577, 16 U.S.C. 1131–1136, 88th Congress, Second Session, September 3, 1964.
4. Földényi, László F. *Melancholy*, trans. Tim Wilkinson (New Haven: Yale University Press, 2016), 71. Sue Halpern sidesteps melancholy while exploring the relationship between privacy and solitude in *Migrations to Solitude* (New York: Pantheon, 1992).
5. Földényi, *Melancholy*, 76.
6. Földényi, 306.
7. Földényi, 322.
8. Ralph Waldo Emerson to John Muir, February 5, 1872, in *The Letters of Ralph Waldo Emerson*, ed. Eleanor M. Tilton, vol. 10 (New York: Columbia University Press, 1995), 68.
9. John Berger, *Ways of Seeing* (London: Penguin, 1972), 34. Walter Benjamin, *Illuminations: Essays and Reflections*, ed. Hannah Arendt, trans. Harry Zohn (New York: Schocken Books, 1968), 217–51.
10. John Berger, "Walter Benjamin" in *Selected Essays*, ed. Geoff Dyer (New York: Pantheon, 2001), 186.
11. Walter Benjamin, "The Storyteller" in *Illuminations*, 83–109, 91–92. "The storyteller: he is the man who could let the wick of his life be consumed completely by the gentle flame of his story. This is the basis of the incomparable aura about the storyteller. . . . The storyteller is the figure in which the righteous man encounters himself" (108–9).

12. Richard White recently commented on the memoir of a distasteful American political figure, Henry F. Bowers, that he "summoned memories to validate things that never happened, not an uncommon trait in memoirs." *The Republic for Which It Stands* (New York: Oxford University Press, 2017), 547.

13. Cees Nooteboom, *Rituals*, trans. Adrienne Dixon (New York: Harvest Books, 1996), 1.

14. Douwe Draaisma, "Memoria: Memory as Writing," in *Metaphors of Memory: A History of Ideas about the Mind*, trans. Paul Vincent (Cambridge: Cambridge University Press, 2000), 17–44.

15. John Muir, *Our National Parks* (Boston: Houghton Mifflin, 1901), 77–78.

16. John Muir, *My First Summer in the Sierra* (Boston: Houghton Mifflin, 1911), 310, 273.

17. "Biodiversity, Yosemite," National Park Service and Delphi International, 2003, https://www.nature.nps.gov/air/edu/someair/parks/yose/IIC1a2.html. Elaine F. Leslie, "A Bold Strategy for Biodiversity Conservation," *Park Science* 31, no. 1 (2014): 6–7, https://www.nps.gov/articles/parkscience31_1_6-7_leslie_3772.htm.

18. Rachel Golden Kroner, Roopa Krithivasan, and Michael Mascia, "Effects of Protected Area Downsizing on Habitat Fragmentation in Yosemite National Park (USA), 1864–2014," *Ecology and Society* 21, no. 3 (2016), http://dx.doi.org/10.5751/ES-08679-210322. Maria J. Santos, Adam B. Smith, James H. Thorne, and Craig Moritz, "The Relative Influence of Change in Habitat and Climate on Elevation Range Limits in Small Mammals in Yosemite National Park, California, USA," *Climate Change Responses* 4, no. 7 (2017), https://doi.org/10.1186/s40665-017-0035-6.

19. "Selection of Colors and Patterns for Geologic Maps of the U.S. Geological Survey," U.S. Geological Survey, U.S. Department of the Interior, last modified December 2, 2016, https://pubs.usgs.gov/tm/2005/11B01/05tm11b01.html.

20. Clement Greenberg once announced, "Because flatness was the only condition painting shared with no other art, Modernist painting oriented itself to flatness as it did to nothing else." "Modernist Painting," *Forum Lectures* (Washington, DC: Voice of America, 1960). Rpt. in *Art & Literature*, no. 4 (Spring 1965): 193–201.

21. The National Park Service has published a wealth of information about the "Geologic Resources Inventory Publications" in a variety of places, including the set of materials here, last updated on February 28, 2018, https://nature.nps.gov/geology/inventory_embed/gre_publications

.cfm. One might consider this material to be advertising since maps are like advertising in a variety of ways, as Arthur M Robinson suggests in *The Look of Maps: An Examination of Cartographic Design* (Madison: University of Wisconsin Press, 1952).

22. Mark Twain, *The Adventures of Huckleberry Finn* (New York: Harper and Brothers, 1912), 405.

23. Brigid Hillebrand, *Climbing the Landscape: Mt. Arapiles—Explorations in Place and the Printed Image* (PhD diss., Monash University, 2016). https://figshare.com/articles/Climbing_the_landscape_Mt_Arapiles_-_explorations_in_place_and_the_printed_image/4696849. Also, see P. A. Nettlefold and E. Stratford, "The Production of Climbing Landscapes-as-Texts," *Australian Geographical Studies*, 37 (1999): 130–141. Jillian M. Rickly, "The (Re) Production of Climbing Space: Bodies, Gestures, Texts," *Cultural Geographies* 24, no. 1 (2017): 69–88.

24. Peter Browning, *Yosemite Place Names: The Historic Background of Geographic Names in Yosemite National Park* (Lafayette, CA: Great West Books, 2005).

25. Steve Roper, *The Climber's Guide to the High Sierra* (San Francisco: Sierra Club Books, 1976), 62–63.

26. Susan R. Schrepfer, "Place Naming in the High Sierra," in *Nature's Altars: Mountains, Gender, and American Environmentalism* (Lawrence: University Press of Kansas, 2005), 15–39.

27. Mark David Spence, "Yosemite Indians and the National Park Ideal, 1916–1969," in *Dispossessing the Wilderness: Indian Removal and the Making of the National Parks* (New York: Oxford University Press, 1999), 115–132, 5, 131.

28. Gary Fields, profile on Department of Communication website, UC San Diego, http://communication.ucsd.edu/people/faculty/gary-fields.html.

29. I recommend two exemplary—and opposed—perspectives on Yosemite: Rebecca Solnit's *Savage Dreams: A Journey into the Hidden Wars of the American West* (San Francisco: Sierra Club Books, 2014), and Alfred Runte's more traditionally argued *Yosemite: The Embattled Wilderness* (Lincoln: University of Nebraska Press, 1990).

30. Draaisma, *Metaphors of Memory*, 11–13.

Chapter 1: Invocation: Going to Granite

1. Ronald Wayne Kistler, *Geologic Map of the Mono Craters Quadrangle, Mono and Tuolumne Counties, California.* US Geological Survey No. 462, 1966.

2. Chiura Obata, *Lake Basin in the High Sierra*, 1930, color woodcut on paper, Smithsonian American Art Museum, Washington, DC, https://americanart.si.edu/artwork/lake-basin-high-sierra-54549.

3. David Brower and Susan R. Schrepfer, *Environmental Activist, Publicist, and Prophet: Oral History Transcript and Related Material, 1974–1980* (Regional Oral History Office, Bancroft Library, University of California, 1980), 94, https://archive.org/details/environmental actoobrowrich.

Chapter 2: Human Bodies

1. Benedictus de Spinoza, *Ethics*, in *The Collected Works of Spinoza*, vol. 1, ed. and trans. Edwin Curley (Princeton, NJ: Princeton University Press, 1985), 21.

2. Philip J. Greaney, "Less is More: American Short Story Minimalism in Ernest Hemingway, Raymond Carver, and Frederick Barthelme" (PhD thesis, Open University, 2005), http://ethos.bl.uk/OrderDetails.do?uin=uk.bl.ethos.424591

3. James A. Whitney, "The Origin of Granite: The Role and Source of Water in the Evolution of Granitic Magmas," *Geological Society of America Bulletin* 100, no. 12 (1988), 1886–97.

4. Gary Snyder, *The Practice of the Wild* (Berkeley, CA: Counterpoint Press, 2010), 110.

Chapter 3: Granite Intrudes

1. *Encyclopaedia Britannica Online*, s.v. "Intrusive rock," accessed March 22, 2018, https://www.britannica.com/science/intrusive-rock.

2. N. King Huber, *The Geologic Story of Yosemite National Park*, US Geological Survey Bulletin 1595 (Washington, DC: U.S. Government Printing Office, 1987), 19–21, http://www.yosemite.ca.us/library/geologic_story_of_yosemite/.

3. Andrew B. Vistelius, "Ideal Granite and its Properties. I. The Stochastic Model," *Journal of the International Association for Mathematical Geology* 4, no. 2 (June 1972): 89–102, https://doi.org/10.1007/BF020 80295. See also Vistelius, *Principles of Mathematical Geology* (Berlin: Springer Science and Business Media, 1992).

4. W. S. Pitcher, *The Nature and Origin of Granite*, 2nd ed. (London: Chapman and Hall, 1997), 17, xv.

5. Bernard Barbarin, "A Review of the Relationships between Granitoid Types, their Origins and their Geodynamic Environments," *Lithos* 46,

no. 3 (1999): 605–26, https://doi.org/10.1016/S0024-4937(98)00085-1. B. Ronald Frost, Calvin G. Barnes, William J. Collins, Richard J. Arculus, David J. Ellis, and Carol D. Frost, "A Geochemical Classification for Granitic Rocks," *Journal of Petrology* 42, no. 11 (2001), 2033–48, https://doi.org/10.1093/petrology/42.11.2033.

6. John Cage tells the following story: "Before studying Zen, men are men and mountains are mountains. While studying Zen, things become confused. After studying Zen, men are men and mountains are mountains. After telling this, Dr. Suzuki was asked, 'What is the difference between before and after?' He said, 'No difference, only the feet are a little bit off the ground.'" *Silence* (Middletown, CT: Wesleyan University Press, 1961), 88.

7. Paul C. Bateman, *Plutonism in the Central Part of the Sierra Nevada Batholith, California*, US Geological Survey Professional Paper 1483 (Washington, DC: U.S. Government Printing Office, 1992), https://pubs.er.usgs.gov/publication/pp1483.

8. Excerpt from Garry Hayes, ed., *The Living Geology of the Sierra Nevada, Great Valley and Coast Ranges of California: A Guidebook* (Modesto, CA : Modesto Junior College, 1998), np. See also Bateman, *Plutonism*.

9. Paul Thrush and the U.S. Bureau of Mines, *Dictionary of Mining, Mineral, and Related Terms*, 2nd ed. (Alexandria, VA: American Geological Institute, 1997).

10. Drew S. Coleman, Walt Gray, and Allen F. Glazner, "Rethinking the Emplacement and Evolution of Zoned Plutons: Geochronologic Evidence for Incremental Assembly of the Tuolumne Intrusive Suite, California," *Geology* 32, no. 5 (2004): 433–36, https://doi.org/10.1130/G20220.1. See also Roger Putnam et al., "Plutonism in Three Dimensions: Field and Geochemical Relations on the Southeast Face of El Capitan, Yosemite National Park, California," *Geosphere* 11, no. 4 (2015): 1133–57, https://doi.org/10.1130/GES01133.1.

11. Craig H. Jones, *The Mountains that Remade America: How Sierra Nevada Geology Impacts Modern Life* (Berkeley: University of California Press, 2017), 127.

12. W. S. Pitcher, *The Nature and Origin of Granite*, 2nd ed. (London: Chapman and Hall, 1997), 20.

13. E. H. T. Whitten, "Granitoid Suites," *Geological Journal* 26, no. 2 (April/June 1991): 117–122, https://doi.org/10.1002/gj.3350260203.

14. Pitcher, *Nature and Origin of Granite*, 343, fig. 19.1.

15. H. H. Read, *The Granite Controversy: Geological Addresses Illustrating the Evolution of a Disputant* (New York: Interscience, 1957), 430.

16. Louise Erdrich, "Two Languages in Mind, but Just One in the Heart," Writers on Writing, *New York Times*, May 22, 2002.

17. William R. Dickinson, "Evolution of the North American Cordillera," *Annual Review of Earth and Planetary Sciences* 32 (2004): 13–45, 25, https://doi.org/10.1146/annurev.earth.32.101802.120257. See also Dickinson, "The Coming of Plate Tectonics to the Pacific Rim," in *Plate Tectonics: An Insider's History of the Modern Theory of the Earth*, ed. Naomi Oreskes and Homer Eugene LeGrand (Boulder, CO: Westview Press, 2001), 264–88.

18. Breck R. Johnson and Allen F. Glazner, "Formation of K-feldspar Megacrysts in Granodioritic Plutons by Thermal Cycling and Late-Stage Textural Coarsening," *Contributions to Mineralogy and Petrology* 159, no. 5 (2010): 599–619, https://doi.org/10.1007/s00410-009-0444-z.

19. George Gaylord Simpson, *Life of the Past: An Introduction to Paleontology* (New Haven: Yale University Press, 1953), 125.

Chapter 4: Up and Down: Mountains Walking

1. Edward Hoagland, "In Praise of John Muir," in *Hoagland on Nature: Essays* (Guilford, CT: Lyons Press, 2003), 442.

2. Dōgen, *Shobogenzo: The True Dharma-Eye Treasury*, trans. Gudo Wafu Nishijima and Chodo Cross, vol. 1 (Berkeley, CA: Numata Center for Buddhist Translation and Research, 2007).

3. Joseph Amata, *On Foot: A History of Walking* (New York: New York University Press, 2004). Frédéric Gros, *A Philosophy of Walking*, trans. John Howe (New York: Verso, 2014). Rebecca Solnit, *Wanderlust: A History of Walking* (London: Penguin, 2001).

4. Leslie Stephen, *The Playground of Europe* (1871; repr., London: Longmans, Green, 1909), 68.

5. Robert Lowell, *New Selected Poems*, ed. Katie Peterson (New York: Farrar, Straus and Giroux, 2017), 102.

6. Herman Melville, *Moby-Dick; or, The Whale* (London: Constable, 1922; Bartleby.com, 2013), http://www.bartleby.com/91/35.html.

7. Moncure Daniel Conway, *Emerson at Home and Abroad* (Trübner, 1883), 306.

8. This text is dated 1932 and begins with the sentence, "The word 'shattered' [or concussion, agitation, vibration, shock: *Erschütterung*] has been used ad nauseam." Walter Benjamin, "Downhill," in *Selected*

Writings, eds. Marcus Bullock and Michael W. Jennings, vol. 2
(Cambridge, MA: Belknap Press, 1996), 593.
9. Gary Snyder, *Practice of the Wild*, 121.

Chapter 5: Glacial Polish

1. John Muir, *Our National Parks* (New York: Houghton Mifflin, 1917), 94.
2. Josiah Dwight Whitney to G. J. Brush, July 10, 1863, in *Life and Letters of Josiah Dwight Whitney*, ed. Edwin Tenney Brewster (New York: Houghton Mifflin, 1909), 230–32.
3. Elizabeth Stone O'Neill, *Meadow in the Sky: A History of Yosemite's Tuolumne Meadows Region* (Fresno, CA: Panorama West Books, 1983), 16–21. See also "National Park Service Cultural Landscape Inventory 2007: Tuolumne Meadows Historic District Yosemite National Park," https://www.nps.gov/yose/learn/historyculture/upload/Tuolumne -Meadows-CLI-lo-res.pdf.
4. John Muir, "Yosemite Glaciers," *New York Tribune*, December 5, 1871.
5. S. Siman-Tov et. al., "The Coating Layer of Glacial Polish," *Geology* 45, no. 11 (2017): 987–90, https://doi.org/10.1130/G39281.1.
6. François E. Matthes, "The Scenery about Tenaya Lake," in *François Matthes and the Marks of Time: Yosemite and the High Sierra* (San Francisco: Sierra Club, 1962). http://www.yosemite.ca.us/library /matthes/tenaya_lake.html.
7. Siman-Tov et. al., "The Coating Layer of Glacial Polish," 989.
8. François E. Matthes, *Geologic History of the Yosemite Valley*, US Geological Survey Professional Paper 160 (Washington, DC: US Government Printing Office, 1930), 129, https://pubs.er.usgs.gov /publication/pp160. This is *the* monumental work by Matthes.

Chapter 6: Signs of Exfoliation and Change

1. David Cort, "Mountaineers: Dilettantes of Suicide," *The Nation*, May 18, 1963, 423–24.
2. Greg M. Stock et al., "Quantitative Rock-Fall Hazard and Risk Assessment for Yosemite Valley, Yosemite National Park, California," US Geological Survey Scientific Investigations Report 2014–5129 (2014), http://dx.doi.org/10.3133/sir20145129. His popular coauthored publication with Allen F. Glazner is *Geology Underfoot in Yosemite National Park* (Missoula: Mountain Press, 2010).
3. Brian D. Collins and Greg M. Stock, "Rockfall Triggering by Cyclic Thermal Stressing of Exfoliation Fractures," *Nature Geoscience* 9 (2016): 395–400, https://doi.org/10.1038/ngeo2686.

4. J. David Rogers, "Overview of PhD Research Sierra National Forest" (web page), accessed March 22, 2018, http://web.mst.edu/~rogersda/phd_research/sierra_nf.htm

5. Gerard Manley Hopkins, *Poems: The First Edition*, ed. Robert Seymour Bridges and William Henry Gardner (Oxford: Oxford University Press, 1961), 94.

6. Marin Cruz Smith, *Polar Star* (New York: Ballantine Books, 1989), 212.

7. Hard to know how old this folk song is; it is named "Rambler, Gambler," "The Moonshiner," "Rose of Aberdeen," or "Roll in my Sweet Baby's Arms."

8. Grove Karl Gilbert, "Domes and Dome Structures of the High Sierra," *Bulletin of the Geological Society of America* 15 (1904): 29–36.

9. For the distinction between exfoliation and sheeting—"exfoliaton follows topography," but sheeting is deeper—see Dov Bahat, Avinoam Rabinovitch, and Vladimir Frid, *Tensile Fracturing in Rocks: Tectonofractographic and Electromagnetic Radiation Methods* (Berlin: Springer Science and Business Media, 2005), 180, 250.

10. Stephen J. Pyne, *Grove Karl Gilbert: A Great Engine of Research* (Iowa City: University of Iowa Press, 2007), 220.

11. See the sidebar "Yosemite in Time: Photographs as Stratigraphic Layers," in Robert H. Webb, *Repeat Photography: Methods and Applications in the Natural Sciences* (Washington DC: Island Press, 2010), 38–40.

Chapter 7: Grace on Granite

1. Gary Snyder, *Riprap and Cold Mountain Poems* (Berkeley, CA: Counterpoint Press, 2009), 8.

2. Robinson Jeffers, *The Selected Poetry of Robinson Jeffers*, ed. Tim Hunt (Stanford, CA: Stanford University Press, 2001), 181.

3. Vladimir Sorokin, *Ice Trilogy*, trans. Jamey Gambrell (New York: New York Review Classics, 2007), 35.

4. J. Hillis Miller, *Topographies* (Stanford, CA: Stanford University Press, 1995), 7.

5. Jeffers, *Selected Poetry*, 24.

6. See David B. Williams, "Rock or Stone: Is There a Difference?" (blog post), GeologyWriter.com, http://geologywriter.com/blog/stories-in-stone-blog/rock-or-stone-is-there-a-difference/.

7. Lucy R. Lippard, *Undermining: A Wild Ride Through Land Use, Politics, and Art in the Changing West* (New York: New Press, 2014).

8. John Muir, *My First Summer in the Sierra* (Boston: Houghton Mifflin, 1911), 336–37.

9. David Brower, ed. *Gentle Wilderness: The Sierra Nevada.* Text by John Muir, Photographs by Richard Kauffman (San Francisco: Promontory Press, 1967).

10. *Merriam-Webster Medical Dictionary*, s.v. "alexithymia," accessed March 24, 2018, https://www.merriam-webster.com/medical/alexithymia. G. J. Taylor and H. S. Taylor, "Alexithymia," in *Psychological Mindedness: A Contemporary Understanding*, eds. M. McCallum and W. E. Piper (Munich: Lawrence Erlbaum Associates, 1997): 29. Marcus K. Taylor et al., "Factors Influencing Physical Risk Taking in Rock Climbing," *Journal of Human Performance in Extreme Environments* 9, no. 1 (2006): 15–26.

11. T. S. Eliot, "Tradition and the Individual Talent," *The Sacred Wood* (Mineola: Courier Corporation, 1997), 33.

12. Jared Farmer, *On Zion's Mount: Mormons, Indians, and the American Landscape* (Cambridge, MA: Harvard University Press, 2009), 5.

13. The Ansel Adams Gallery, "New Release—Monolith, the Face of Half Dome as Modern Replica," June 27, 2014, http://anseladams.com/new-modern-replica-monolith-face-half-dome/.

14. Mark Carey, M. Jackson, Alessandro Antonello, and Jaclyn Rushing, "Glaciers, Gender, and Science: A Feminist Glaciology Framework for Global Environmental Change Research," *Progress in Human Geography* 40, no. 6 (2016): 770–93. https://doi.org/10.1177/0309132515623368.

15. Susan R. Schrepfer, *Nature's Altars: Mountains, Gender, and American Environmentalism* (Lawrence: University Press of Kansas, 2005), 52.

16. Anne Marie Rizzi, "Hands on Half Dome Quartz Monzonite," in *The Games Climbers Play*, ed. Ken Wilson (London: Hodder and Stoughton, 1978), 479–82.

17. Michael P. Cohen, *The Pathless Way: John Muir and American Wilderness* (Madison: University of Wisconsin Press, 1984). Michael P. Cohen, *The History of the Sierra Club* (San Francisco: Sierra Club, 1988).

Chapter 8: The Transformation of Things

1. Jack Kerouac, *On the Road: The Original Scroll* (New York: Penguin, 1997), np. Allen Ginsberg, "The Voice of Rock" (1948), in *Collected Poems 1947–1997* (New York: Harper Collins, 2010), 18.

2. Poetry Foundation Glossary of Poetic Terms, s.v. "volta," accessed March 24, 2018, https://www.poetryfoundation.org/resources/learning/glossary-terms/detail/volta.

3. *Zhuangzi: Basic Writings*, trans. Burton Watson (New York: Columbia University Press, 2003), 44. According to another translation, "This is called 'things change.'" See Chad Hansen, "Zhuangzi," Stanford

Encyclopedia of Philosophy, December 17, 2014, https://plato.stanford
.edu/entries/zhuangzi/.

4. Jonathan Bate, *The Song of the Earth* (London: Pan Macmillan, 2001),
153.

5. Quoted in Zachary Rosenau, "The Creaturely Language of John Clare"
(blog post), November 8, 2016, https://zacharyrosenau.wordpress.com
/2016/11/08/the-creaturely-language-of-john-clare/.

6. Quoted in Lucas Klein, "Not Altogether an Illusion: Translation and
Translucence in the Work of Burton Watson," *World Literature Today*
(May-August 2014), https://www.worldliteraturetoday.org/2014/may
-august/not-altogether-illusion-translation-and-translucence-work
-burton-watson#.VSSqdPnF_HT. Emphasis added.

7. Maximiliano Korstanje, "The Origin and Meaning of Tourism:
Etymological Study," *e-Review of Tourism Research (eRTR)* 5, no. 5
(2007), http://www.academia.edu/353007/The_Origin_and_Meaning
_of_Tourism_Etymological_Study.

Chapter 9: Out of Bounds

1. Carolyn Cassady, quoted in Andrew O'Hagan, "Jack Kerouac: Crossing
the Line," *New York Review of Book* 60, no. 5 (March 21, 2013).

2. US Geological Survey, *Tuolumne Meadows Quadrangle, California*
[map], 1:62,500. N3745—W11915/15. AMS 2159 IV-Series V795. Denver,
CO: US Geological Survey, 1956.

3. Arthur H. Robinson, *The Look of Maps: An Examination of
Cartography Design* (Madison: University of Wisconsin Press, 1952), 13.

4. Jill Desimini and Charles Waldheim, *Cartographic Grounds: Projecting
the Landscape Imaginary* (Princeton, NJ: Princeton Architectural
Press, 2016), 68.

5. Thoreau's outbursts about stupidity are sprinkled throughout *Walden*.
For example, he speaks of extravagance, ridiculing those who act "as if
Nature could support but one order of understandings . . . As if there
were safety in stupidity alone." *Walden* (New York: New American
Library, 1960), 215.

6. Loren Eiseley, *The Unexpected Universe* (New York: Harcourt Brace
Jovanovich, 1985), 48–67.

Chapter 10: Rock and Water

1. Histories of Tioga Road include Keith A. Trexler, *The Tioga Road:
A History, 1883–1961* (San Francisco: Yosemite Natural History
Association, 1980). http://www.yosemite.ca.us/library/tioga_road/. See

also https://en.wikisource.org/wiki/Tioga_Road_(HAER_No._CA -149)_written_historical_and_descriptive_data.

2. P. A. Nettlefold and E. Stratford, "The Production of Climbing Landscapes-as-Texts," *Australian Geographical Studies* 37 (1999): 130–141. Jillian M. Rickly, "The (Re) Production of Climbing Space: Bodies, Gestures, Texts," *Cultural Geographies* (2016): 69–88. https:// doi.org/10.1177/1474474016649399.

3. N. King Huber, *The Geologic Story of Yosemite Valley: In the Footsteps of François E. Matthes*, US Geological Survey Bulletin 1595 (1922, revised 1929 and 1938), https://geomaps.wr.usgs.gov/parks/yos/topobk.html.

4. Greg Stock and Robert Anderson, "Final Report: Yosemite's Melting Glaciers," (December 2012), http://files.cfc.umt.edu/cesu/NPS/CU /2009/09_11Anderson_YOSE_glaciers_fnl%20rpt.pdf.

5. Wallace S. Broecker, "Was the Medieval Warm Period Global?" *Science* 291, no. 5508 (2001): 1497–1499. Broecker writes, "Using radiocarbon dating and ring counting, Stine has shown that for 70 years before 1093 A.D., the lake stood at least 13 m below its outflow spillway, and for 141 years before 1333 A.D., it stood at least 11 m below its spillway." See also Scott Stine, "Extreme and Persistent Drought in California and Patagonia during Mediaeval Time," *Nature* 369, no. 6481 (1994): 546–549. https:// doi:10.1038/369546a0. Scott Stine, "Medieval Climatic Anomaly in the Americas," in *Water, Environment and Society in Times of Climatic Change*, eds. Arie S. Issar and Neville Brown. (Dordrecht: Springer, 1998): 43–67. https://doi.org/10.1007/978-94-017-3659-6_3. Scott Stine, "Climate Change in Wildland Management: Taking the Long View," *Proceedings of the Sierra Nevada Science Symposium*, eds. Dennis D. Murphy and Peter A. Stine (Albany, CA: Pacific Southwest Research Station, Forest Service, US Department of Agriculture, 2004), 51–55.

6. T. S. Eliot, *The Waste Land*, ed. Michael North, A Norton Critical Edition (New York: Norton, 2001), 6, 16, 17.

7. Martin J. S. Rudwick, *Bursting the Limits of Time: The Reconstruction of Geohistory in the Age of Revolution* (Chicago: University of Chicago Press, 2005), 307, 314, 363.

8. Rudwick, *Bursting the Limits of Time*, 326.

9. Rudwick, *Bursting the Limits of Time*, 586.

10. Andrew Wagner, "Scientists Have Discovered 4.2 Billion-Year-Old Remnants of the Earth's First Crust," PBS Newshour, March 16, 2017, http://www.pbs.org/newshour /rundown/scientists-discovered-4-2 -billion-year-old-remnants-Earths-first-crust/.

11. John B. Jackson, *Discovering the Vernacular Landscape* (New Haven: Yale University Press, 1984), 156.

12. John B. Jackson, *Landscape in Sight: Looking at America* (New Haven: Yale University Press, 2000), xxi.

13. Linda W. Greene, "Chapter 10: Significant Historical Properties in Yosemite National Park," in *Yosemite: the Park and its Resources; a History of the Discovery, Management, and Physical Development of Yosemite National Park, California* (Denver: National Park Service, 1987). http://www.yosemite.ca.us/library/yosemite_resources /properties.html.

14. National Park Service Cultural Landscapes Inventory 2007, Tuolumne Meadows Historic District, Yosemite National Park, September 13, 2007. https://www.nps.gov/yose/learn/management/upload/Final -TMDistrict-CLI-09-13-07.pdf.

15. "Tuolumne Meadows Mess Hall (Visitors Center) – Yosemite National Park CA," The Living New Deal website, Department of Geography, University of California, Berkeley, accessed April 11, 2018, https://living newdeal.org/projects/tuolumne-meadows-mess-hall-visitor-center -yosemite-national-park-ca/.

16. John W. Bingaman, *Pathways: A Story of Trails and Men* (Lodi, CA: Endkian, 1968).

17. Anne Whiston Spirn, "Constructing Nature," in *Uncommon Ground: Rethinking the Human Place in Nature*, ed. William Cronon (New York: Norton, 1996), 95.

Chapter 11: Inside Rock

1. Albert Camus, *The Myth of Sisyphus and Other Essays* (New York: Knopf, 1955).

2. Voltaire, *"Sept Discours en Vers sur l'Homme,"* 1738.

3. William Cronon, "The Trouble with Wilderness: or, Getting Back to the Wrong Nature," and Richard White, "Are You an Environmentalist or Do You Work for a Living," in *Uncommon Ground*, ed. William Cronon (New York: Norton, 1995). Citing White and Jennifer Price, Cronon writes, "It is not much of an exaggeration to say that the wilderness experience is essentially consumerist in its impulses" (481n37).

4. Joseph Campbell, *The Power of Myth*, with Bill Moyers, ed. Betty Sue Flowers (New York: Anchor, 1988), 113.

5. Jack Kerouac, *The Dharma Bums* [1958] (New York: Penguin Books, 1976), 33.

6. See Vali Memeti, Scott R. Paterson, and Keith D. Putirka, *Formation of*

NOTES 207

the Sierra Nevada Batholith: Magmatic and Tectonic Processes and their Tempos (Boulder, CO: Geological Society of America, 2014).

7. Wallace Stevens, "No Possum, No Sop, No Taters," in Collected Poems [1943] (New York: Vintage Press, 1990), 293–94.

Chapter 12: Right and Wrong Kinds of Rock

1. Jon Krakauer, "Country Rock" in Home Ground: Language for an American Landscape, eds. Barry Lopez and Debra Gwartney (San Antonio, TX: Trinity University Press, 2010), 88.
2. David Craig, Native Stones: A Book about Climbing (London: Martin Secker and Warbug, 1987), 9.
3. Rudwick, Bursting the Limits of Time, 95.
4. Gary Snyder, "Piute Creek," Riprap and Cold Mountain Poems (Berkeley, CA: Counterpoint Press, 2009), 8.
5. Congressman William Kent on Muir, quoted in Roderick Nash, Wilderness and the American Mind (New Haven: Yale University Press, 1967), 174.

Chapter 13: An Aristotelian Mythology of Geohistory

1. William R. Dickinson, "The Place and Power of Myth in Geoscience: An Associate Editor's Perspective," American Journal of Science 303 (November 2003): 856–64. https:// doi:10.2475/ajs.303.9.856.
2. Rudwick, Bursting the Limits of Time, 16.
3. When I was young, the standard history of the Sierra Nevada was Francis P. Farquhar's History of the Sierra Nevada (Berkeley: University of California Press, 1965). This history emphasized a narrative of European exploration and recreation. More recently, David Beesley, in Crow's Range: An Environmental History of the Sierra Nevada (Reno: University of Nevada Press, 2004), focuses on environmental issues. Craig H. Jones, in The Mountains That Remade America: How Sierra Nevada Geology Impacts Modern Life (Berkeley: University of California Press, 2017), focuses more on geology and promotes the use of geological determinism. Also, for climbing, see Joseph E. Taylor, Pilgrims of the Vertical: Yosemite Rock Climbers and Nature at Risk (Cambridge, MA: Harvard University Press, 2010).
4. William Carlos Williams, The Collected Poems of William Carlos Williams, vol. 2, 1939–1962, ed. Christopher MacGowan (New York: New Directions, 1988), 55.
5. See Yvon Chouinard and Tom Frost, "A Word . . . " and Doug Robinson, "The Whole Natural Art of Protection," in the 1972 Chouinard Catalog: 2–3, 12–13, reproduced online by R.A. Hutchins, http://www.climbaz.com/chouinard72/chouinard.html.

Chapter 14: The Purity of Granite

1. Julia Franz and Charlie Berquist, "Before Plate Tectonics, the Earth May Have Been Covered by One Giant Shell," Science Friday, Public Radio International, March 27, 2017, https://www.pri.org/stories/2017 -03-27/plate-tectonics-Earth-may-have-been-covered-one-giant-shell.

2. Tim E. Johnson, et al., "Earth's First Stable Continents did not Form by Subduction," *Nature* 543, no. 7644 (2017): 239–42. https://doi:10.1038 /nature21383.

3. Kent C. Condie and Alfred Kröner, "When did Plate Tectonics Begin? Evidence from the Geologic Record," *Geological Society of America Special Papers* 440 (2008): 281–94. https://doi.org/10.1130/2008.2440(14).

4. Peter Anthony Cawood, C. J. Hawkesworth, and B. Dhuime, "The Continental Record and the Generation of Continental Crust," *Geological Society of America Bulletin* 125, no. 1-2 (2013): 14–32; 14, 32. https://doi.org/10.1130/B30722.1.

5. Pitcher, *Nature and Origin of Granite*, 320. See also John D. Clemens, Fernando Bea, eds., *Granite Petrogenesis*, Mineralogical Society Landmark Papers Volume 4 (Middlesex, UK: Mineralogical Society of Great Britain and Ireland, 2012).

6. Michael Brown, "The Contribution of Metamorphic Petrology to Understanding Lithosphere Evolution and Geodynamics," *Geoscience Frontiers* 5, no. 4 (2014): 553–69. https://doi.org/10.1016 /j.gsf.2014.02.005.

7. For the volcanic-plutonic connection, see A. F. Glazner, D. S. Coleman, R. D. Mills, "The Volcanic-Plutonic Connection," *Advances in Volcanology* (Berlin: Springer, 2015). Also Carl R. Anhaeusser, "Archaean Greenstone Belts and Associated Granitic Rocks—A Review," *Journal of African Earth Sciences* 100 (2014): 684–732. https://doi.org/10.1016/j .jafrearsci.2014.07.019.

Chapter 15: A Contingent Earth

1. Jack Morrell, "Homeric Geologists," review of *Bursting the Limits of Time* and *Worlds Before Adam*, by Martin Rudwick, *Notes and Records, The Royal Society Journal of the History of Science*, March 11, 2009, https://doi.org/10.1098/rsnr.2009.0012.

2. Rudwick, *Worlds Before Adam*, 2.

3. Minoru Ozima, *Geohistory: Global Evolution of the Earth* (Berlin: Springer-Verlag, 1987), 1. See also his "Changes in the Earth's Crust," *Geohistory* (Berlin: Springer, 1987): 99–131.

4. Rudwick, *Worlds Before Adam*, 566.

5. Rudwick, *Worlds Before Adam*, 557.

6. Rudwick, *Worlds Before Adam*, 557, 563.

7. S. J. Martel, "Effect of Topographic Curvature on Near-Surface Stresses and Application to Sheeting Joints," *Geophysical Research Letters* 33 (2006), L01308. https://doi.org/10.1029/2005GL024710. S. J. Martel, "Formation of Sheeting Joints as a Result of Compression Parallel to Convex Surfaces, With Examples from Yosemite National Park, California," *AGU Fall Meeting Abstracts* 1 (2008).

Chapter 16: Myths of Glaciers

1. Edward D. Ives, *George Magoon and the Down East Game War: History, Folklore, and the Law* (Urbana-Champaign: University of Illinois Press, 1993), 10.

2. Bruce Jackson, "Conversations with Leslie A. Fiedler: Newark, Jews and the Boy on the White Horse," *CounterPunch* (January 3–4, 2004).

3. N. King Huber, "The Late Cenozoic Evolution of the Tuolumne River, Central Sierra Nevada, California," *Geological Society of America Bulletin* (1990): 102–115; 102. https://doi.org/10.1130/0016-7606(1990) 102<0102:TLCEOT>2.3.CO;2.

4. Julie Cruikshank, *Do Glaciers Listen? Local Knowledge, Colonial Encounters, and Social Imagination* (Vancouver: University of British Columbia Press, 2014).

5. Gary Snyder, *Riprap and Cold Mountain Poems* (Berkeley: Counterpoint, 2009), 9–10.

6. Bill Guyton, *Glaciers of California: Modern Glaciers, Ice Age Glaciers, the Origin of Yosemite Valley, and a Glacier Tour in the Sierra Nevada* (Berkeley: University of California Press, 1998), 38–39.

7. Cruikshank, *Do Glaciers Listen?*, 175.

Chapter 17: Erratics, Domes, and Trundling

1. Tobias Krüger, *Discovering the Ice Ages: International Reception and Consequences for a Historical Understanding of Climate* (London: Brill, 2013): 23–24.

2. Personal correspondence, October 1, 2015.

3. Jason Groves, *Erratic: Fictions of Movement in Goethe, Stifter, and Benjamin* (PhD diss., Yale University, 2012), 98, https://pqdtopen .proquest.com/pubnum/3525212.html.

4. Jason Groves, "Goethe's Petrofiction: Reading the Wanderjahre in the Anthropocene," Goethe Yearbook 22, no. 1 (2015): 95–113. https://doi .org/10.1353/gyr.2015.0018.

5. "Striations, Roche Moutonnée and Craig and Tail," The Geography Site, November 29, 2008, http://www.geography-site.co.uk/pages/physical/glaciers/stria.html.

6. S. F. Forrester, "The Rucksack Club Journal" (1931), reprinted in *The Games Climbers Play,* ed. Ken Wilson (London: Hodder and Stoughton, 1978), 411–18.

Chapter 18: Iconic Landscape

1. "Granite," Yosemite National Park California, National Park Service website, August 30, 2016, https://www.nps.gov/yose/learn/nature/granite.htm.

2. Richard A. Becker et al., "Preexisting Fractures and the Formation of an Iconic American Landscape: Tuolumne Meadows, Yosemite National Park, USA," *GSA Today* 24, no. 11 (2014): 1. https://doi.org/10.1130/GSATG203A.1.

3. Matthes, *Geologic History of the Yosemite Valley,* 15.

4. Richard A. Becker et al., "Preexisting Fractures and the Formation of an Iconic American Landscape: Tuolumne Meadows, Yosemite National Park, USA," *GSA Today* 24, no. 11 (2014): 4. https://doi.org/10.1130/GSATG203A.1.

5. John Ott, *Manufacturing the Modern Patron in Victorian California: Cultural Philanthropy, Industrial Capital, and Social Authority* (Burlington, VT: Ashgate, 2014).

6. Trexler, The Tioga Road, www.yosemite.ca.us/library/tioga_road/automobiles_arrive.html.

7. Ursula K. Heise, *Sense of Place and Sense of Planet: The Environmental Imagination of the Global* (New York: Oxford University Press, 2008), 55.

8. Heise, *Sense of Place and Sense of Planet,* 10.

9. Steven and Mary Thompson, *Wild Food Plants of the Sierra* (Berkeley, CA: Wilderness Press, 1976).

10. "Park Statistics," Yosemite National Park California, National Park Service website, April 5, 2018, https://www.nps.gov/yose/learn/management/statistics.htm. Ariel Blotkamp et al., *Yosemite National Park Visitor Study Summer 2009* (Park Studies Unit, Report 215), https://www.nps.gov/yose/learn/nature/upload/Visitor-Use-Summer-2009-Study.pdf.

11. Ulrich Beck, "The Cosmopolitan Society and its Enemies," *Theory, Culture and Society* 19, no. 1-2 (2002): 17–44. https://doi.org/10.1177/026327640201900101. As Beck argues, "'Cosmopolitanism' means—as Immanuel Kant argued 200 years ago—being a citizen of two worlds—'cosmos' and 'polis.' There are five different dimensions to this, distinguishing

between external and internal otherness. Externally it means: (a) including the otherness of nature; (b) including the otherness of other civilizations and modernities; and (c) including the otherness of the future; internally it means: (d) including the otherness of the object; and (e) overcoming the (state) mastery of (scientific, linear) rationalization" (18).

12. Ulrich Beck, *The Cosmopolitan Vision,* trans. Ciaran Cronin (Malden, MA: Polity, 2006), 3.

13. Becker et al., "Preexisting Fractures," 1, 9.

Chapter 19: The Sound of Talus

1. James Gleick, *Chaos: Making a New Science* (New York: Penguin, 1988), 103–107.

2. "Faces in Nature Pareidolia and Mimetoliths," Facebook page, https://www.facebook.com/Mimetoliths.Pareidolia/.

3. David Hume, *The Natural History of Religion,* with an introduction by John M. Robertson (London: Bradlaugh Bonner, 1889; South Australia: University of Adelaide ebooks, 2014). https://ebooks.adelaide.edu.au/h/hume/david/h92n/section3.html.

4. Doug Robinson, "Running Talus," Great Pacific Iron Works Catalog (1975): 65–70. See http://www.edhartouni.net/great-pacific-ironworks-1975.html.

5. David Sellars, "Rock Garden Design: Stratified or Chaotic?" *Rock Garden Quarterly* 65, no. 1 (2007), 12.

Chapter 20: Fairview Dome

1. John Muir, *The Yosemite* (New York: Century, 1912), 178–180. https://vault.sierraclub.org/john_muir_exhibit/writings/the_yosemite/chapter_11.aspx

2. Grove Karl Gilbert, "Domes and Dome Structure of the High Sierra," *Geological Society of America* Bulletin 15, no. 1 (1904): 29–36; 35.

3. US Geological Survey, "Feature Detail Report for: Fairview Dome," USGS Geographic Names Information System, December 31, 1981, https://geonames.usgs.gov/apex/f?p=gnispq:3:0::NO::P3_FID:253464.

4. Gilbert, "Domes and Dome Structure," 29.

5. Jay Taylor, "Mapping Adventure: A Historical Geography of Yosemite Valley Climbing Landscapes," *Journal of Historical Geography* 32, no. 1 (2006): 190–219; 195, 213. https://doi.org/10.1016/j.jhg.2004.09.002.

6. Jones, *The Mountains That Remade America,* 118. Jones cites Miriam Dühnforth, Robert S. Anderson, Dylan Ward, and Greg M. Stock, "Bedrock Fracture Control of Glacial Erosion Processes and Rates," *Geology* 38, no. 5 (2010): 423–426. https://doi.org/10.1130/G30576.1.

7. Jones, *The Mountains That Remade America,* 121.

8. Becker et al., "Preexisting Fractures," 1, 9.

Chapter 21: Above and Below: Ghosts of Glaciers

1. F. Solgadi and E. W. Sawyer, "Formation of Igneous Layering in Granodiorite by Gravity Flow: A Field, Microstructure and Geochemical Study of the Tuolumne Intrusive Suite at Sawmill Canyon, California," *Journal of Petrology* 49, no. 11 (2008): 2009–2042. https://doi.org/10.1093/petrology/egn056.

2. M.D. Higgins, "Origin of Megacrysts in Granitoids by Textural Coarsening: A Crystal Size Distribution (CSD) Study of Microcline in the Cathedral Peak Granodiorite, Sierra Nevada, California," in *Understanding Granites: Integrating Modern and Classical Techniques,* eds. C. Fernandez and A. Castro, Special Publication 158 (London: Geological Society of London, 1999), 207–219.

Chapter 22: Meandering Around Matthes Crest

1. Reid V. Moran, "Matthes Crest," *Sierra Club Bulletin* 34 (1949): 110–11.

2. François Matthes, "Cockscomb Crest," *Sierra Club Bulletin* 11, no. 1 (1920): 21–28, reprinted in François Matthes and the Marks of Time, 83. http://www.yosemite.ca.us/library/matthes/cockscomb_crest.html.

3. Matthes, "Cockscomb Crest," 81.

4. François Matthes, *The Incomparable Valley: A Geological Interpretation of the Yosemite* (Berkeley: University of California Press, 1950), 28.

5. Matthes, *Geologic History of the Yosemite Valley,* 64.

6. N. King Huber, *The Geologic Story of Yosemite National Park,* http://www.yosemite.ca.us/library/geologic_story_of_yosemite/final_evolution.html.

Chapter 23: The View from Pothole Dome

1. Grove Karl Gilbert, "Moulin Work under Glaciers," *Bulletin of the Geological Society of America* 17 (1906): 317–320.

2. US Geological Survey, "Glossary of Glacier Terminology," s.v. "Moulin," http://pubs.usgs.gov/of/2004/1216/text.html#m.

3. Richard Balogh, "Where Water Flowed 'Uphill' on Pothole Dome," *Yosemite Nature Notes* 46, no. 2 (1977): 34–39. http://www.yosemite.ca.us/library/yosemite_nature_notes/46/2/pothole_dome.html. See also "Pothole Dome - Glacial Features," Geocaching website, https://www.geocaching.com/geocache/GC1QN2J_pothole-dome-glacial-features. John Muir, *Studies in the Sierra,* ed. William E. Colby (San Francisco: Sierra Club Books, 1960), 12.

4. Clarence King, *Mountaineering in the Sierra Nevada* (Boston: James Osgood, 1872), 328.

5. G. V. Dal Piaz and W. G. Ernst, "Areal Geology and Petrology of Eclogites and Associated Metabasites of the Piemonte Ophiolite Nappe, Breuil—St. Jacques Area, Italian Western Alps," Tectonophysics 51, no. 1-2 (1978): 99–126. https://doi.org/ 10.1016/0040-1951(78)90053-7.

6. See "Details for Benchmark HR2743," Geocaching website, https:// www.geocaching.com/mark/details.aspx?PID=HR2743.

Chapter 24: Granite at Sunrise

1. Mary Hill, *Geology of the Sierra Nevada* (Berkeley: University of California Press, 1975), 179–202.

2. On the western edge of the Tuolumne Intrusive Suite, geologists notice the dramatic change in granitic rocks and increasing complexity, yet because the glacial sculpturing seduces the walker by easy transport from one region or another, these are not immediately apparent. See Brendon L. Johnson, "Structure, Construction, and Emplacement of the Yosemite Valley Intrusive Suite and the Yosemite Creek Granodiorite in the Central Sierra Nevada Batholith" (master's thesis, San Jose State University, 2013). http://scholarworks.sjsu.edu/etd_theses/4280.

3. Herman Melville, "Chapter LXXIX: The Prairie," *Moby Dick; or, The Whale* (London: Constable, 1922; Bartleby.com, 2013), http://www .bartleby.com/91/79.html.

4. Jones, *The Mountains That Remade America*, 123–24.

5. John Muir, *The Mountains of California,* Chapter 1.

6. Mike Strickler, "What do the terms mafic and felsic mean?," Ask GeoMan, GeoMania, http://jersey.uoregon.edu/~mstrick/AskGeoMan /geoQuerry11.html; "What are the most important types of rock in the crust?," Ask GeoMan, GeoMania, http://jersey.uoregon.edu/~mstrick /AskGeoMan/geoQuerry27.html.

7. "15 Breathtaking Views of The World That Will Make You Dizzy with Wonder," Bright Side, https://brightside.me/article/15-breathtaking -views-of-the-world-that-will-make-you-dizzy-with-wonder-26305/.

8. Sally Ann Ness, *Choreographies of Landscape: Signs of Performance in Yosemite National Park* (New York: Berghahn Books, 2016).

Chapter 25: This is Not a Mountain

1. Geoffrey C. Bowker, *Memory Practices in the Sciences* (Cambridge, MA: MIT Press, 2005), 36.

2. Bowker, *Memory Practices in the Sciences,* 7, 230.

3. "Sierra Nevada Batholith Geologic Map Mosaic," University of North Carolina at Chapel Hill, http://geomaps.geosci.unc.edu/quads/quads .htm. See photos on "Geology Documentary—History Channel 12/22/09" discussion thread, Supertopo, http://www.supertopo.com /climbing/thread.php?topic_id=1037429&tn=140.

4. Geoffrey C. Bowker and Susan Leigh Star, *Sorting Things Out: Classification and its Consequences* (Cambridge, MA: MIT Press, 2000), 1, 10.

5. "Geological History of Earth—Granite?" discussion thread, Supertopo, http://www.supertopo.com/climbing/thread.php?topic_id =731799&msg=732325#msg732325.

6. Minerals notes common minerals found in granitic rock: Quartz – SiO_2; Potassium feldspar (Orthoclase) – $KAlSi_3O_8$; Plagioclase feldspar (Albite – Anorthite) – $NaAlSi_3O_8$ – $CaAlSi_3O_8$; Biotite – $K(Mg,Fe)_3(Al,Fe)SiO_{10}(OH,F)_2$; Hornblende – $(Ca,Na)_{2\text{-}3}(Mg,Fe_{+2},Fe_{+3},Al)_5(Al,Si)8O_{22}(OH)$; Titanite – $CaTiSiO_5$; Magnetite – Fe_3O_4; Apatite – $Ca_5(PO_4,CO_3)_3(F,OH,Cl)$; Garnet (Almandine) – $Fe_3Al_2(SiO_4)_3$; Muscovite – $KAl_2(AlSi_3)O_{10}(OH)_2$; Ilmenite – $FeTiO_3$; Monazite – $(Ce,La,Nd,Th) PO_4$; Zircon – $ZrSiO_4$; Tourmaline – $(Na,Ca)(Mg,Fe_{+2},Fe_{+3},Al,Mn,Li)_3Al_6 (BO_3)_3(Si_6O_{18})(OH,F)_4$.

7. Ronald Wayne Kistler, *Structure and Metamorphism in the Mono Craters Quadrangle, Sierra Nevada, California*, Geological Survey Bulletin 1221-E (Washington, DC: US Government Printing Office, 1966). https://pubs.usgs.gov/ bul/1221e/report.pdf. Ronald Wayne Kistler, *Geologic Map of the Mono Craters Quadrangle, Mono and Tuolumne Counties, California*. Geologic Quadrangle 462. (USGS, 1966). https://pubs.er.usgs.gov/publication/gq462.

Chapter 26: Granite As Enigma

1. Herbert Harold Read, *The Granite Controversy: Geological Addresses Illustrating the Evolution of a Disputant* (London: Murby, 1957).

2. Antonio Castro, "The Off-Crust Origin of Granite Batholiths," *Geoscience Frontiers* 5, no. 1 (2014): 63–75; 63, 64. https://doi.org/10.1016/j.gsf.2013.06.006.

3. Edward Abbey, "Author's Introduction," *Desert Solitaire* (New York: McGraw-Hill, 1968), xiii.

4. Gaia Vince, *Adventures in the Anthropocene: A Journey to the Heart of the Planet We Made* (New York: Random House, 2014), 299.

5. Siim Sepp, "Composition of the Crust," Sandatlas, http://www.sand atlas.org/composition-of-the-Earths-crust/.

6. Jeremy Davies, *Birth of the Anthropocene* (Berkeley: University of California Press, 2016), 195.

Chapter 27: An Edge of History: An Edge of a Continent

1. Huber, *The Geologic Story of Yosemite National Park*, 54. http://www
.yosemite.ca.us/library/geologic_story_of_yosemite/final_evolution.html.

2. Huber, *The Geologic Story of Yosemite National Park*, 53. See also Ronald
W. Kistler, *Structure and Metamorphism in the Mono Craters Quadrangle*.

3. See Matthes, "The Geologic History of Mount Whitney," François
Matthes and the Marks of Time. http://www.yosemite.ca.us/library
/matthes/mount_whitney.html.

4. Jones, *The Mountains That Remade America*, 189.

5. Elna Bakker, *An Island Called California: An Ecological Introduction to Its
Natural Communities* (Berkeley: University of California Press, 1971), xi.

6. Karin Sigloch and Mitchell G. Mihalynuk, "Intra-Oceanic Subduction
Shaped the Assembly of Cordilleran North America," *Nature* 496,
no. 7443 (2013): 50–56. https://doi.org/doi:10.1038/nature12019.

7. "New Study Reveals Insights on Plate Tectonics," UCLA Newsroom,
March 3, 2014, http://newsroom.ucla.edu/releases/new-insights-on
-plate-tectonics-250174; Caroline Beghein et al., "Changes in Seismic
Anisotropy Shed Light on the Nature of the Gutenberg Discontinuity," *Science*
343, no. 6176 (2014): 1237–1240. https://doi.org/10.1126/science.1246724.

8. Jones, *The Mountains That Remade America*, 189.

9. P. W. Rundel and C. I. Millar, "Alpine Ecosystems," in *Ecosystems of
California. Berkeley, California*, eds. E. Zavaleta and H. Mooney
(Berkeley: University of California Press, 2016), 613–34.

10. Christian Körner, *Alpine Plant Life: Functional Plant Ecology of
High Mountain Ecosystems* (Berlin: Springer Science and Business
Media, 2003). Jianguo Chen et al., "How Cushion Communities Are
Maintained In Alpine Ecosystems: A Review And Case Study On
Alpine Cushion Plant Reproduction," *Plant Diversity* (2017): 221–28.
https://doi.org/10.1016/j.pld.2017.07.002.

11. John Muir, John of the Mountains: *The Unpublished Journals of John
Muir* (Madison: University of Wisconsin Press, 1979), 205.

12. David Robertson, *Real Matter* (University of Utah Press, 1997), 100.

13. Jack Kerouac, *The Dharma Bums*, 206.

14. Paul Wienpahl, *The Matter of Zen* (New York: New York University
Press 1964), 105.

15. Royal Robbins, *To Be Brave* (Ojai, CA: Pink Moment Press, 2009).
Qtd in Benjamin Kirk, "Royal Robbins, legendary Yosemite climber
and clothing manufacturer, has died," KFSN TV Fresno (March 15,
2017). http://abc30.com/news/royal-robbins-legendary-yosemite
-climber-and-clothing-manufacturer-has-died-/1802234/.

Epilogue: Ventifacts

1. Herman Melville, "Bartleby the Scrivener," in *The Piazza Tales* (Evanston, IL: Northwestern University Press, 1987), 43.

2. N. T. Bridges et al., "Ventifacts at the Pathfinder Landing Site," *Journal of Geophysical Research: Planets* 104, no. E4 (1999): 8595–615. https://doi.org/10.1029/98JE02550.

3. Samuel Taylor Coleridge, "The Eolian Harp," line 44–48.

4. "What is Suiseki?," Suiseki.com, http://suiseki.com/about/index.html.

5. Massimo Leone, "Nature and Culture in Visual Communication: Japanese Variations on Ludus Naturae," *Semiotica* 2016, no. 213 (2016): 213–245. https://doi.org/10.1515/sem-2015-0145.

6. Jim Perrin, *Mirrors in the Cliffs, The Games People Play* vol. 2 (Birmingham, AL: Menasha Ridge Press, 1983).

7. Emmanuel Levinas, *Humanism of the Other*, trans. Nidra Poller (Urbana-Champaign: University of Illinois Press, 2003), 12.

Acknowledgments

When you are climbing on rock, you do not ask yourself philosophical questions. Later, questions constitute a different matter. We run on rock. Water runs on rock. We rock. As it turns out, granitic rocks are very literary minerals, belonging, as they do, to letters or learning.

I have learned a great deal from granite and over the years enjoyed the privilege to live many summers in Tuolumne Meadows, surrounded by these granitic texts. Now, I seek granite anywhere I find it: I try to touch it every day. Where I now spend my summers, this is an easy enterprise, right out my back door. Down the road, two giant erratic boulders sit next to the fire station, one perched on top of the other. So it is with the people I love. We were not born here, born to rock, but we were drawn to the rock so that it seems like home.

I could name a rock for every one of my early climbing partners, most of them still alive:

Valerie, of course; Sigma Alpha, Eric Beck, Ken Boche, Roy Coates, Gary Colliver, Bud Couch, Jeff Dozier, Dick Erb, Nick Estcourt, Tom Gerughty, Ivan Getting, Richard Goldstone, Dennis Hennek, Mort Hemple, Tom Higgins, T. M. Herbert, Tom Kimbrough, Don Lauria, Elaine Matthews, Russ McLean, Chuck Pratt, Frank Sarnquist, George Sessions, Claude Suhl, Steve Thompson, Chris Vandiver, and many more. I do not take these names of my friends in vain. From each I learned a great deal.

We have been unusually fortunate to become part of a seasonal community in Tuolumne Meadows, encouraged for many years by Margaret Eissler, who established the Parsons Memorial Lodge Summer Series, an annual forum for the arts and sciences.

Michelle Niemann has been the best editor I could hope for. Like my first editor, Sam Allen, she has been a better judge than I. Justin Race, our publisher, has consistently encouraged our literary pursuits. Everything I write has to pass Valerie's stringent judgment.

Gary Snyder's exemplary writing is behind almost all of my own efforts. I received help and encouragement for this project by Jon Christensen, Jason Groves, Craig Jones, and Shalev Siman-Tov. In the longer term, what I have written here continues a long discussion with many historians and literary scholars, including, but not limited to, Michael Branch, William Cronon, Terry Gifford, Cheryll Glotfelty, Ursula Heise, Patricia Limerick, Tom Lyon, Sean O'Grady, Scott Slovic, Jay Taylor, Richard White and Donald Worster. This book breaks almost all the conventions of these discussions and its transgressions can only be attributed to my own un-teachable impulses.

About the Author

MICHAEL P. COHEN grew up in Southern California's San Fernando Valley, was educated at UCLA, UC Riverside, and UC Irvine. He taught for 27 years at Southern Utah University. Between 2000 and 2005, he was visiting professor in Literature and Environment at the University of Nevada, Reno.

His first book, *The Pathless Way: John Muir and American Wilderness*, won the Mark H. Ingraham Prize from the University of Wisconsin Press, among other awards. He has been a research fellow of the National Endowment of Humanities, a Danforth Fellow, and was awarded a Distinguished Teaching Award by the Utah Academy of Sciences, Arts, and Letters. His *The History of the Sierra Club 1892–1970* has been called "a rare book: an institutional history that is nonetheless balanced, impartial, and unsparingly honest." His recent book, *A Garden of Bristlecone Pines: Tales of Change in the Great Basin,* was published by the University of Nevada Press and was a Finalist for Western States Book Award (WESTAF) in nonfiction. In 2017, he co-authored *Tree Lines* with Valerie P. Cohen, also published by the University of Nevada Press.

He has written an influential essay, "Blues in the Green: Ecocriticism under Critique," for *Environmental History* (2004), that explores the groundings of Ecocriticism, in the historically changing ideas of ecology, evolutionary theory, and literary theory, in the context of the environmental politics of the late twentieth century.

He is known in the academic world as a pioneer in the realms of environmental history and "ecocriticism." His writing is directed not only toward academic audiences: His western history has the literary qualities of fiction and his writings on trees are accessible histories of science. His work radiates a passion for the western landscapes.

Cohen also has a distinguished record as a rock climber and mountaineer. He is a pioneer of first ascents in the Sierra Nevada and has been a professional mountain guide. His work is marked by familiarity with the wild rivers and mountains of the west and informed by varied and multidisciplinary scholarly interests.

He first visited Tuolumne Meadows in 1955.